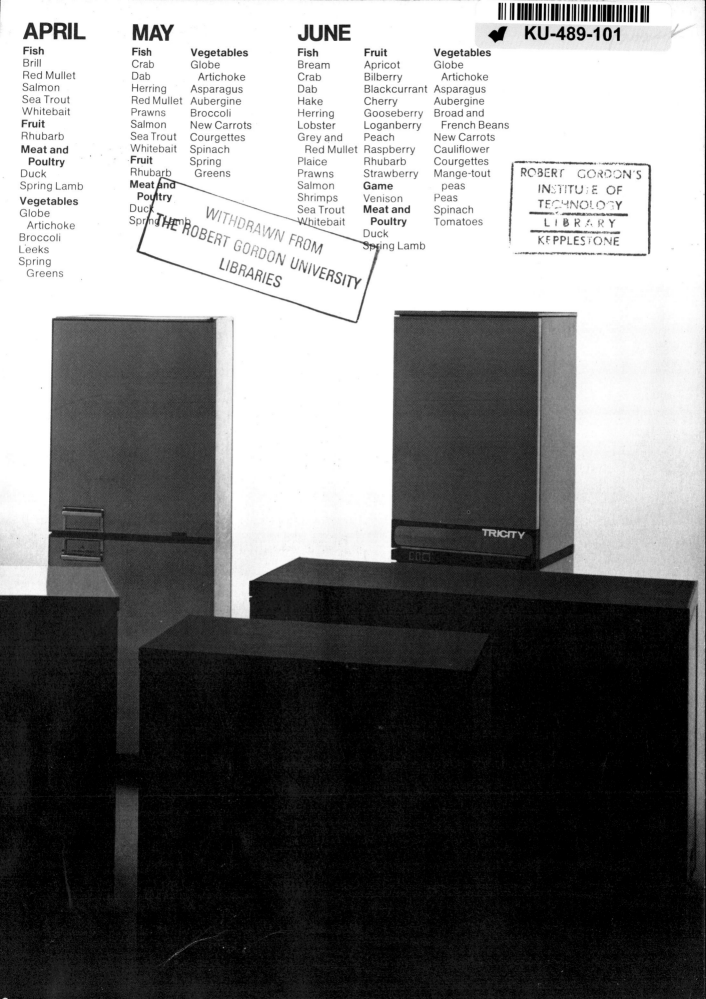

APRIL

Fish
Brill
Red Mullet
Salmon
Sea Trout
Whitebait
Fruit
Rhubarb
**Meat and
  Poultry**
Duck
Spring Lamb
Vegetables
Globe
  Artichoke
Broccoli
Leeks
Spring
  Greens

MAY

Fish
Crab
Dab
Herring
Red Mullet
Prawns
Salmon
Sea Trout
Whitebait
Fruit
Rhubarb
**Meat and
  Poultry**
Duck
Spring Lamb

Vegetables
Globe
  Artichoke
Asparagus
Aubergine
Broccoli
New Carrots
Courgettes
Spinach
Spring
  Greens

JUNE

Fish
Bream
Crab
Dab
Hake
Herring
Lobster
Grey and
  Red Mullet
Plaice
Prawns
Salmon
Shrimps
Sea Trout
Whitebait

Fruit
Apricot
Bilberry
Blackcurrant
Cherry
Gooseberry
Loganberry
Peach
Raspberry
Rhubarb
Strawberry
Game
Venison
**Meat and
  Poultry**
Duck
Spring Lamb

Vegetables
Globe
  Artichoke
Asparagus
Aubergine
Broad and
  French Beans
New Carrots
Cauliflower
Courgettes
Mange-tout
  peas
Peas
Spinach
Tomatoes

THE FREEZER BOOK

THE FREEZER BOOK

Marye Cameron-Smith

Elm Tree Books in association with Hamish Hamilton Limited

First published 1973 in Great Britain
by Elm Tree Books Limited
90 Great Russell Street London WC1
Second Impression January 1974

Copyright © 1973
Marye Cameron-Smith

SBN 241 02282 7

Recipe testing and food preparation
by Valerie Edwards, Tricity Test Kitchen,
Thorn Domestic Appliances (Electrical) Limited

Book layouts and decorations by
Norma Crockford

Photographs by Paul Radkai

Accessories by courtesy of
David Mellor Ironmonger and
Selfridges Limited

Printed in Great Britain by
Sir Joseph Causton & Sons Limited,
London and Eastleigh.

CONTENTS

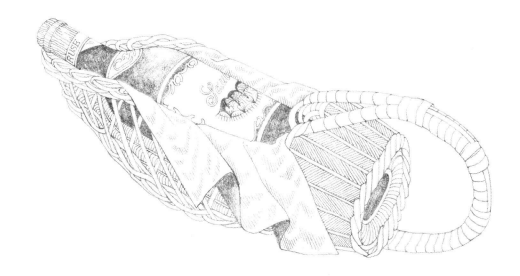

INTRODUCTION

More than any other household appliance, the freezer can make a valuable contribution to raising the standard of living of the average family: it can save a good deal of time through cutting down the number of shopping trips; purchasing in large quantities can cut down food-bills enormously, whether for fresh foods to be frozen at home or ready-frozen products to be stored; far greater advantage may be taken of top-quality seasonal specialities while their prices are low; cooking and baking sessions can be embarked upon as and when *you* find it convenient—which isn't necessarily just before a meal-time; wholesome and attractive dishes may be prepared well in advance, fast frozen, then quickly heated and served in the minimum space of time should unexpected guests arrive or in case of similar emergency! Above all, the freezer can ensure that whether you are a busy housewife with a large family or whether you live entirely alone, you will live better by eating better, with a choice of food to your own liking always available.

Imaginative housewives can give many meals their own creative touch to please their families in less time than it would take to prepare a more ordinary dish. All in all, it's no wonder that freezer owners say they would sooner part with any other home-appliance than lose their freezer!

BASIC PRINCIPLES OF FREEZING FOOD

Early man's preoccupation was finding food, but in today's world the problem has changed to that of preserving wholesome food in such a way that the natural flavour, colour, texture and nutritional value are retained for relatively long periods of time. Among today's methods of food preservation are drying, salting, pickling, canning, and sterilisation, but the technique which maintains the good eating qualities of most foods best, i.e. closest to that of the original food, is freezing.

Although natural ice was available in winter to early man, its value was not appreciated; however, he did eventually discover that fresh food could be kept for a short while if stored in natural caves, especially those of volcanic origin, which were dry and cool. It was quite a time before men realised that moisture and warmth were the principal causes of the rapid deterioration of good food, and started using ice to cool the air in food stores.

The first household 'refrigerators' were probably the 'ice houses' built in the grounds of some country houses during the eighteenth century. Natural ice, collected from a nearby lake or stream in the winter months, was stored for many months in large, brick-lined, egg-shaped holes in the ground and later used for preserving food in the kitchen. The top of the igloo-shaped ice house above ground was usually kept shaded from the sun by trees planted on the south side of it. The discovery of mechanical refrigeration to make ice available all the year round led to the replacement of natural ice and to the first household refrigerators with controlled cold-air temperature, in which food could be stored for a few days.

If cold air at temperatures just above that of the melting point of ice would keep food wholesome for a short time, then a more intense cold, much lower than the freezing point of water should preserve food in good condition for a much longer period of time. So reasoned Clarence Birdseye, the American explorer who noted that fish caught through holes in the Labrador ice and frozen in the cold arctic temperature was virtually indistinguishable from freshly-caught fish, even after it had been lying in the arctic ice for many months.

This fish retained its natural flavour and texture because it was really fresh at the time of freezing, had been cooled very quickly, covered in a 'glaze' of ice to prevent it drying and held at a steady low temperature. These are the basic principles of successful freezing of food, and mechanical refrigeration provides not only the means of preserving food in cool air for a short time, but one of the most important and now one of the most popular techniques of food-processing. So freezing food, both in the factory and at home, is a simple and a safe way of preserving food, as well as being the most natural.

COMMERCIAL FREEZING

After a slow start in the 1920s, when the quality of commercially frozen food was poor as a result of slow rather than quick freezing, the frozen-food companies began using the centuries-old tradition of the Eskimos, and soon developed the art of quick freezing to a high degree of sophistication. The first lesson they learnt was that reducing the temperature of fresh food to $-18°C$ ($0°F$) over a long period of time resulted in a product of poor eating quality, especially through loss of the original texture. It is particularly important, in home freezing as well as commercial, to reduce the temperature of the food as rapidly as possible between the $-1°$ to $-5°C$ range ($30°$ to $23°F$) and to recognise that the freezing process is only complete when the temperature of the warmest part of the food has been cooled to $-18°C$ ($0°F$). Water, the major component of most foods, contains the soluble cell components which make up the characteristics of different foods. By reducing the temperature quickly through the zone of maximum crystallisation ($-1°$ to $-5°C$), the water is converted into a large number of small ice crystals, without damaging the cell walls. At slow rates of freezing, taking many hours, the ice crystals grow to a relatively large size throughout this temperature range, and the water diffuses through the cell walls, which leads to mechanical damage and a consequent deterioration of the texture and the structure of the food. By the time the food has been cooled to $-18°C$ ($0°F$), most of the 'free' water in the food has been frozen.

For the same reason, it is important for the

food to pass quickly through the zone of maximum crystallisation when it is being thawed ready for eating, or for use as a recipe-ingredient. The quick-freezing refrigeration equipment used by the commercial frozen-food companies is therefore designed to decrease the temperature of food very quickly and freeze it to as low as –34°C (–30°F). Thus the good eating qualities are preserved and long-period storage is no problem.

FOOD FREEZERS AND CONSERVATORS

In the same way, a food freezer is specially designed to freeze food, and though it will not freeze food as quickly, or to such a low temperature, as the costly commercial equipment, it will freeze fast enough to ensure that the desirable qualities of good food are retained, as long as the basic principles are followed. It is therefore important to buy a genuine food or home freezer which will freeze a stated quantity of food within twenty-four hours and to avoid an appliance which has been designed and is *only intended to store food which has already been frozen*. Attempts to freeze fresh food in conservators, storage cabinets or star-marked frozen-food storage compartments in household refrigerators are likely to result in slow freezing. Not only will the food, once frozen, be of poor quality but, during the long freezing period, any food already frozen and being stored may rise in temperature for a relatively long time, which could easily cause *that* to deteriorate in quality too.

FROZEN-FOOD STORAGE COMPARTMENTS

Most frozen-food storage compartments built into household refrigerators now being sold are marked with either one, two or three six-pointed stars located in a curved frame. This marking gives an indication of the time of storage of commercially frozen food. A one-star marking on the compartment door means that most frozen foods can be stored for up to one week, (ice-cream for up to one day); two stars up to one month, (ice-cream for up to one week); three stars up to three months (ice-cream up to one month).

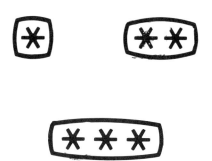

This marking therefore refers to the time of food storage, and appliances carrying these markings alone are normally unsuitable for freezing fresh food. Food freezers or home freezers, as they are popularly called, will store commercially frozen food for up to three months but will also remove heat from fresh food quick enough to fast-freeze without any significant change in the quality of any frozen food being stored in the appliance.

THE CHOICE OF FOOD FREEZERS

The distinguishing symbol for freezers, introduced in 1973, is a rectangular frame containing a large six-pointed star and three smaller six-pointed stars in a curved frame. The large star symbolises the food freezing capacity and three small stars (the same as those used on frozen food storage compartments) indicate that most commercially frozen foods can be stored for up to three months.

When this new symbol is used, the manufacturers must state, in the instructions for use, the maximum weight of food that can be frozen in twenty-four hours.

Leaving aside now storage cabinets and star-marked storage compartments, there is a wide choice of food freezers which vary in size from about 4 cubic feet to about 20 cubic feet capacity. If frozen food is tightly packed in (and depending upon the type of food), each cubic foot of space will hold between 18 and 20 pounds of frozen food. In the past, it has been common practice to assess the size of freezer required by allowing 2 cubic feet per person in the family, but the popularity of home freezing and sales of commercially frozen food are now developing so rapidly that 3 or even 4 cubic feet per person would be a more realistic basis—the higher figure especially for those families having easy access to sea-fresh fish, market gardens and high-class butchers. Once the size

has been considered, the type of freezer can be decided upon and this will mainly depend upon the space available for its installation.

There are three types of food freezer from which to choose: the chest, the upright and the refrigerator-freezer (sometimes called a 'combination'). Providing that an assurance has been given that they are genuine food freezers, each type has its own characteristics and advantages. The decision as to which type is best will almost always depend upon the space available to accommodate it but obviously the kitchen, where food is normally prepared and stored, would be the first choice. Some of the convenience of a home freezer is lost if it has to be inconveniently located.

CHEST FREEZERS

This type of freezer occupies the greatest floor space for each cubic foot of capacity and, as the name implies, it is fitted with a lift-up lid. It may be inconvenient to use the lid as a work-top or storage surface because anything on top must be removed to gain access inside. However, this may not be important if the freezer is to be installed in a well ventilated dry pantry or in an outhouse. The best of the chest freezers are fitted with a 'fast freeze' switch and a separate 'fast freeze' compartment where packaged fresh foods are placed for freezing, before being transferred to the main storage section. A counter-balanced lid with lock, interior lighting, indicator lights to show satisfactory operation and with fitted baskets as standard are all desirable and convenient features to look for when making a final choice of

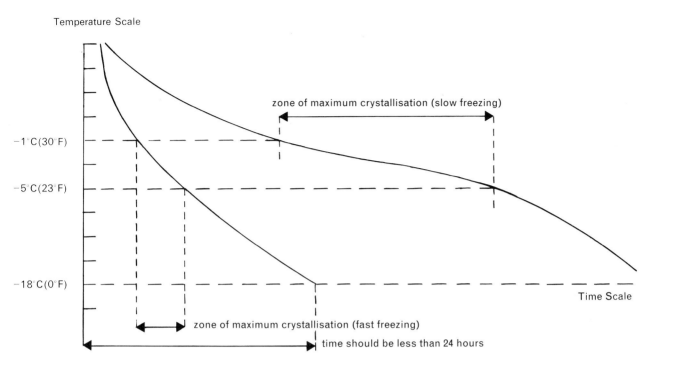

FROZEN FOOD TEMPERATURE CHART

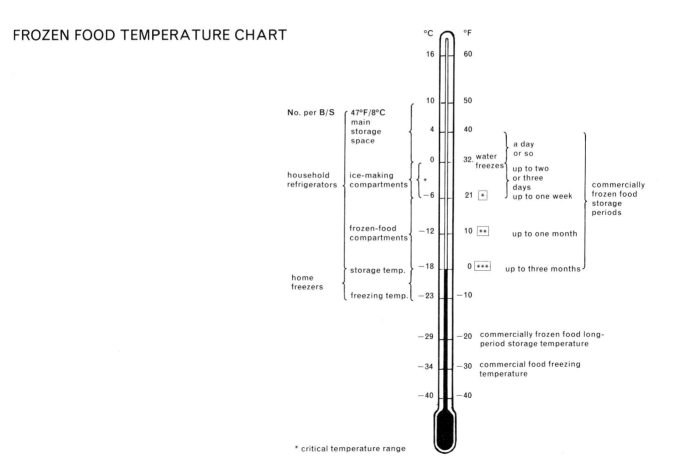

* critical temperature range

temperature of frozen food inside during a short door-opening. However, if the door is left open for long periods, more frequent defrosting will be needed because warm air entering the freezer at the top to replace the cold air falling out will carry with it water vapour, which will become frost and ice on the refrigerated shelves and walls of the freezer. The best of the larger-capacity upright freezers are fitted with two doors, which reduces the loss of cold air. If there is any doubt about the strength of the floor on which upright freezers (or refrigerator-freezers) are to stand, the total weight of the loaded freezer can be estimated by adding the weight of the empty freezer to the weight of food it will hold, allowing 25 pounds of food for each cubic foot of space (this will include a small safety margin).

this type of freezer. Access to particular packages, especially in the deep part of the chest, is not so convenient nor so easy as when using an upright freezer.

UPRIGHT FREEZERS

This type is growing in popularity because upright freezers occupy a smaller floor area for each cubic foot of storage space—important when the freezer is to be installed in a kitchen. These front-opening freezers provide quick access to food located on shelves and in quickly removable small baskets. Like chest freezers, the best are equipped with 'fast freeze' switches, 'fast freeze' compartments and indicator lights. When the door is opened, some cold air, being heavier than the air surrounding the freezer, falls out, but this is relatively unimportant and does not affect the

REFRIGERATOR-FREEZERS ('Combinations')

For those whose kitchen space is a critical factor, the recently introduced wide range of refrigerator-freezers may make this a compulsive choice. Quite frequently a new refrigerator-freezer, combining half refrigerator space for chilled foods and half low-temperature space for frozen foods, will stand on the same floor area as that of a refrigerator alone. All that is required is the additional height. The attraction of this combination is that chilled and frozen foods are stored in one place in the kitchen or pantry—an important advantage to the busy housewife.

RUNNING COSTS

An approximation of the cost of running a home freezer can be made by allowing between 2 and 4 units of electricity per cubic foot per week and there is little difference between the three types. The actual cost will depend much more upon the frequency of batches of food put in for freezing, the number of door openings and the location of the freezer.

STYLE AND PERFORMANCE

The choice of style and finish is now so varied that it is no longer necessary to accept a traditional white paint finish. Progressive food freezer manufacturers have already made available elegant freezers styled and finished to tone in with contemporary kitchen furniture. Whichever size and type seem to be most appropriate, appliances carrying the British Electrotechnical Approvals Board mark are strongly recommended for this ensures compliance with minimum standards of safety and durability, and a performance up to current British Standard specifications.

HINTS FOR THE FREEZER

Having decided where the freezer can be located most conveniently, it is worth while checking that it is level. Some freezers are fitted with adjustable feet—others may require some durable packing material to level up the cabinet if the floor is uneven. The big advantage of levelling is to ensure that the lid on a chest freezer or the door on an upright cabinet will close evenly on the seal and avoid air leakages. A faulty door seal will rapidly increase the need to defrost and, in extreme cases, may cause the refrigerating system to operate continuously and perhaps fail to cool the interior to the correct low temperature.

The location chosen should be well ventilated to allow a passage of air through the refrigerating unit compartment and around the back of an upright model, if fitted with a wire condenser on the back panel. The running cost will be minimised if the freezer is in a cool, but not damp, location. If it has to be in a cellar, garage or outhouse and there is a risk of dampness, the freezer can stand on blocks of hardwood and regular cleaning of the exterior is advisable.

POWER SUPPLY

The 13 amp or equivalent 3-pin power point to which the freezer is connected can be taped over if there is any risk of it being switched off or disconnected accidentally. This risk is, of course,

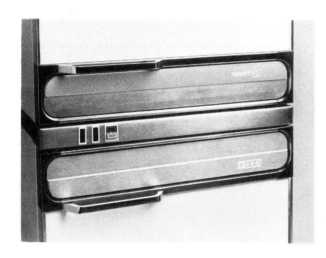

INSURANCE

Most freezer manufacturers give a one-year guarantee on the new complete freezer including the refrigerating system. The contents, however, can be valuable too and it is possible to insure against loss or damage to frozen food caused by power or mechanical failure. Premiums start at around £2.00 per £100 worth of food insured, but may be less if the Insurance Company already covers a household comprehensive policy. Insurance groups will insure the contents of freezers but, if advice is needed, contact the Food Freezer Committee, 25 North Row, London W.1.

considerably reduced with freezers which are fitted with an indicator light system. If there is a failure of the electricity supply, the door or lid of the freezer should be kept closed and the temptation to look inside should be resisted. Power cuts rarely last long enough to cause a significant rise in food temperature, especially if the freezer is well stacked with tightly packed food. The more frozen food there is in store, the longer it will take to soften. It is advisable to keep the door or lid closed for a couple of hours after the power supply has been restored. Any frozen food, be it home or commercially frozen, can be successfully re-hardened if it has softened, without any disastrous loss of quality. However, any food which has thoroughly thawed should be treated as normal perishable food and used within an appropriate time. Alternatively, raw vegetables, meat or fish can be used soon after thawing, as ingredients in a recipe, and refrozen after cooking.

FREEZERS IN USE

Many owners find it helpful to keep a thermometer in their freezer and there are inexpensive models which are especially suitable. A circular thermometer with a $2\frac{1}{2}$-inch dial in a strong metal frame, incorporating a spring clip, is compact and ideal. It can be clipped to a shelf or basket or on one of the inner door shelves. During normal storage, the air temperature inside the freezer should not be warmer than –18°C (0°F) and, when freezing a batch of food, the fast-freeze compartment should be as much below –18°C (0°F) as the fast-freeze switch or thermostat control at its coldest setting will provide. Unprotected glass-stemmed thermometers which are more easily broken are not recommended.

Before putting a batch of fresh food to freeze, it is advisable to depress the fast-freeze switch, or to turn the thermostat control to its coldest setting, at least two hours before freezing and then remember to return the switch or thermostat control to its normal position for storage after twenty-four hours. It is uneconomic to operate the freezer at temperatures much colder than –18°C (0°F) with the refrigerating system running continuously.

DEFROSTING

There will come a time, of course, when frost or ice has formed on the interior walls and shelves and the manufacturer's detailed instructions should be followed (there are a few home freezers with automatic defrosting equipment, but as yet these are rather more expensive). Normally, manual defrosting will be needed three or four times a year, depending on how frequently and how long the door or lid has been open and, on these occasions, it is necessary to remove the contents. All frozen food and especially ice-cream should be well protected whilst out of the freezer, and left out for the minimum time possible. Packages on every occasion should be packed tightly together and preferably wrapped in two sheets of aluminium foil: failing that, the next best thing is five or six sheets of newspaper. The ideal place to put the frozen food packages is in the refrigerator, otherwise in as cool a place as possible. Protected in this way, frozen food will retain its high quality for up to an hour, whilst the freezer is defrosted. Make sure the freezer is disconnected from the power supply before defrosting and thoroughly dry the interior before closing the door or lid and switching on again. Then allow the freezer to run for a short while before reloading the frozen food. This is a good time to check the food in store and reload last those packages which have been in longest. Put aside for early use any food which has faulty packaging. And after defrosting, a good quality refrigerator polish used on the exterior, according to the manufacturer's instructions, will keep a freezer looking as new as the day it was installed.

WORTHWHILE PRECAUTIONS

If there is a lock on the freezer door or lid, especially in the case of larger appliances, do keep the keys away from the freezer and well out of reach of children. And then when the time comes to discard a freezer (or refrigerator, for that matter) and to replace it with a new one, make sure that the door or lid fastener is removed or—better still, take the door or lid right off the hinges. Discarded refrigerators and freezers with tightly fitting doors and lids are dangerous playthings for children!

PACKAGING FOOD

No food, with the possible exception of pastry, some say, will improve in quality by home freezing and storage but, if food is really fresh at the time of freezing, it can be successfully stored for long periods; but it must be carefully prepared and then properly packaged. If the recommended storage times are not greatly exceeded, the frozen food will be just as wholesome in colour, flavour and nutritional value as when it was frozen. The low temperature air in a freezer is dry and any food not properly sealed will gradually lose its natural moisture and may develop 'freezer burn'.

This in no way makes the food unsafe but might make some foods unpleasant to eat.

So packaging material used for home freezing should have some important special qualities; it should be:

a   Free from taint and odour
b   Moisture- and vapour-proof, to prevent loss of moisture during low temperature storage
c   A suitable shape to allow fast freezing by keeping individual packages as thin as is practicable
d   Resistant to breaking or cracking at low temperature
e   Flexible so that dry foodstuffs can be tightly wrapped, leaving a minimum amount of air in the package.

These are rather stringent requirements but, fortunately, a wide variety of materials and rigid containers are available at reasonable prices in most large stationers and departmental stores. There are also two companies which specialise in supplies of home freezer packaging and other accessories:

FRIGICOLD LTD
166 Dukes Road, Western Avenue, London W.3.
Tel. 01-993 1271

LAKELAND PLASTICS
102 Alexandra Road, Windermere, Westmorland.
Tel. Windermere 2255

The principal types of packaging, most suitable for food freezing at home, are:

Polythene bags, available in many sizes and suitable for a few portions or bulk quantities of vegetables and fruit, for small cuts of meat, chops, poultry, loaves of bread and pastries.

Polythene sheet, especially useful for interleaving individual portions of fish, chops, beefburgers, etc.

Polythene tubs with lids, for soft fruit, egg yolks and whites, fruit juices, vegetables in sauce, stews and casseroles. Are also useful as moulds after lining with a polythene bag or aluminium freezer foil.

Freezer foil, trays and containers.

Freezer foil can be used for wrapping most types of dry foods and for long storage is best used in double thickness, ensuring that all cut edges are double folded to make an air-tight seal. Foil trays and containers are useful for pies, stews and most other cooked dishes. Use freezer foil to cover the top.

To ensure a moisture- and vapour-proof seal of polythene bags and tubs and for sealing freezer foil, bag ties (polythene or paper covered wire) and freezer tape will be needed. Coloured labels to identify each package before freezing with contents and date are available and have an adhesive which will stick to non-greasy packages even at low temperature.

It is not always essential to store food in the same package in which it was frozen. In many circumstances, it is more convenient not to! Ice cubes can be frozen in refrigerator ice-trays, demoulded and then quickly transferred to a polythene bag for storage in bulk and they will not stick together.

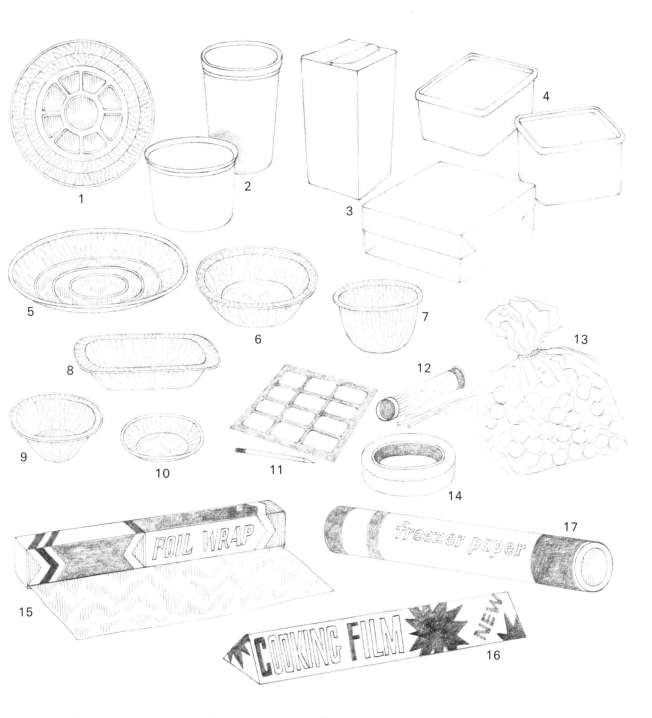

1 Aluminium plate	10 Aluminium tartlet case
2 Waxed tubs	11 Labels
3 Waxed cartons	12 Bag fasteners
4 Plastic containers	13 Plastic bag
5 Large aluminium dish	14 Sealing tape
6 Small aluminium dish	15 Aluminium foil
7 Aluminium pudding basin	16 Transparent cooking film
8 Aluminium pie dish	17 Freeze paper
9 Aluminium baking case	

'Free-flow' packs of frozen strawberries, raspberries, brussels sprouts and other small fruits and vegetables can be produced at home by laying a single layer on a clean baking tray. Placed on a refrigerated shelf in a freezer, they will freeze quickly and individually and can then be transferred in batches to polythene bags or a rigid container and sealed. 'Free-flow' freezing in this way allows just the right quantity of fruit or vegetables to be poured from the bag or container whenever required and the remainder can be resealed and returned to the freezer for future use.

To keep the number of rigid containers to a minimum and so save precious freezer space, oven- and flame-proof dishes or polythene tubs can be lined with an appropriate size of polythene bag or freezer foil. Food for freezing, e.g. stews, casseroles, vegetables in sauces, fruit in sugar and other cooked dishes can then be poured in and the rigid container with contents and a temporary cover of polythene sheet or freezer foil is placed in the freezer. After freezing, the wrapped food can be lifted out of the rigid container, labelled and permanently sealed to go back to the freezer for storage. And the container is then free for normal kitchen use or as a mould for more freezing. Packages frozen in this way can be stacked neatly and tightly together in the freezer, to make most economical use of the storage space available.

Similarly, cooked and uncooked pastries, like mince-pies and tarts, can be frozen in baking tins with a simple foil cover, then removed when frozen and packaged in convenient portions and sealed in compact units.

When wrapping foods which contain sharp bones, it is as well to cover any projecting pieces or sharp points with muslin or greaseproof paper before applying the overwrap which may be freezer foil or polythene. This will help prevent the outer protective wrapping being punctured when the package is frozen. Bags, for reheating foods, made from a special heat-resistant material, which are also suitable for freezing, are now available. Called 'boil-in bags', they can be used as packaging for freezing prepared foods which can later be cooked in boiling water in the same bag and there is the big advantage of cooking from the frozen state.

The type of packaging material used is obviously a matter of personal experience and preference and it will depend upon the shape, quantity and kind of food. Because thin packages will freeze faster than thicker ones, it is preferable to freeze and store several smaller packages rather than one large one—and more convenient to use too. Leave a headspace to allow for expansion when freezing liquids, soups and sauces, otherwise ensure that the wrapping material fits tightly and snugly round other foods to exclude air as much as possible. And finally, wipe packages dry before placing them in the freezer.

Whilst there are some inexpensive substitute materials which can be used—empty cream and yoghourt tubs for example, many waxed paper and plastic materials are not suitable nor are they intended for use in food freezers and, without being sure, it is best to avoid them, especially for foods which are to be stored for any length of time. Having spent time and money in the preparation of some favourite foods, it is very disappointing to find that they have dehydrated, or even developed off-flavours, after storage due to broken packaging, the use of material not moisture- or vapour-proof, or plastic containers which are not suitable for use in freezers.

PACKAGING PRECAUTIONS
If large polythene bags are purchased for later use, keep them well out of the way of children. Don't place sealed containers (especially glass ones) which contain carbonated liquids, fizzy drinks, etc. in low-temperature storage compartments and freezers.

STORAGE LIFE OF HOME-FROZEN FOODS
The storage life recommendations given in the recipe section assume that only really fresh foods have been used as ingredients, that they have been hygienically prepared, packed and sealed and then fast-frozen to the centre of the package within twenty-four hours, then maintained at a steady low temperature not higher than $-18°C$ ($0°F$).

Because different types and varieties of food have different water content, texture and chemical make-up, there is a considerable variation in the storage life after freezing. Generally speaking, foods containing relatively high percentages of fat and/or highly volatile ingredients have a short storage life. Temperature fluctuations of a few degrees above $-18°C$ ($0°F$) for a short time, whilst defrosting for example, if not repeated more than two or three times, will not have any significant effect upon the quality of the food. Most vegetables have a long storage life and are

much more tolerant of fluctuations in temperature than, for example, oily fish and ice-cream, which are heat-sensitive foods and have a relatively short storage life. All the time frozen food is being stored, even at $-18°C$ ($0°F$), it is very slowly changing in flavour, colour and texture. The storage life is chosen by the time it takes these changes to be noticed, when compared with the original food. As the senses of taste and smell vary between one person and another, so one person's opinion of storage life may be different from another's. For this reason storage life can only be given for general guidance.

There is little to be gained from storing frozen foods for very long periods, just for the sake of it. Much better to get the full benefits by freezing food when convenient and eating it when it will be most enjoyed. A food freezer which is frequently used is the one which will give best value for money.

STORAGE LIFE OF COMMERCIALLY FROZEN FOODS
Most manufacturers of commercially quick-frozen foods give a recommended high-quality storage life on each packet. For most quick-frozen foods, the storage life in 3-star compartments and in food freezers is up to three months. For most ice-cream and some dairy and fish products, the storage life is only up to one month. The time is much shorter than the equivalent for home-frozen food, primarily because the bought frozen food has already been stored by the manufacturer for a period of time and also because the food has probably been exposed to small temperature fluctuations during

distribution and during the time between the shop display cabinet and the food freezer. Quick-frozen foods which have softened on the surface (but not thawed) during the carry-home time can be hardened in a food freezer without any consequent change in the recommended storage life. Any foods which have thawed—provided they have not been at high temperatures, i.e. over 10°C (50°F), for a long time—can be refrozen. but there is likely to be some loss of flavour, colour and texture. The storage life will be shortened and the foods will not be so enjoyable to eat.

Bought quick-frozen foods, especially raw vegetables, fruit, fish, poultry and pastry can, of course, be used as ingredients when preparing cooked dishes for home freezing. But it is important that these foods should not have been thawed long enough for normal spoilage to occur and they should be handled hygienically and as little as possible, preferably by cooking them from the frozen state where practicable.

THAWING FROZEN FOODS
Rapid thawing is desirable, for the same reason as fast freezing, especially through the zone of maximum crystallisation. Whenever possible, frozen foods should be cooked from the frozen state. Vegetables, especially, benefit from being plunged into boiling salted water straight from the freezer. Other foods, which are not to be cooked, should thaw whilst still covered at normal kitchen temperature. The amount of juice, or 'drip' as it is called, which runs from food on thawing is an indication of the change in texture caused by slow freezing. The less the 'drip', the better will be the flavour and texture.

The important exceptions to the rule of cooking from the frozen state are foods which are dense and close textured, such as poultry and game. Large chickens, ducks and turkeys, must be thoroughly thawed before cooking, preferably whilst covered in a refrigerator. Poultry of about 14 pounds in weight, for example, will take up to thirty-six hours to thaw through to the centre. Frozen joints and pieces of chicken, to be used as ingredients for stews, casseroles and curries need not be thawed, provided the cooking time is relatively long. A useful tip for frozen cream sponges, fruit tarts and other similar confections, is to cut them into portions whilst they are still relatively hard. This not only reduces the thawing time but results in neat and cleanly sliced portions.

Water ices, e.g., lollies, which most children enjoy, should be allowed to thaw for a few minutes before they are put into the mouth. If consumed immediately after removal from a very low temperature in a freezer, there is a risk that they could 'burn' the tongue.

FOODS FOR THE FREEZER

Home freezing is a natural and simple way of preserving good food which, fortunately, requires no previous experience to achieve complete success. The FOOD FREEZING CALENDAR at the ends of the book is a reminder when to buy and freeze perishable foods, but there are also a few simple rules to follow in the preparation of raw food and cooked dishes, in addition to the usual rules of hygiene.

Freeze only really fresh food—ideally, young fresh vegetables and fruit straight from the garden, picked in the cool temperatures of early morning. Remember also to take advantage of such seasonal specialities as Seville oranges when they are available locally and at their best. Avoid freezing overmature and bruised produce. Prepare fish as for normal cooking, ideally straight after being caught in the sea or river. Cool and package meat, poultry and game as soon as possible after slaughter, hanging and cleaning. Even successful home freezing will only maintain, not improve, the quality and flavour of the original food.

Keep all kinds of food as cool as possible after purchase and when carrying it back home. Avoid handling food any more than is strictly necessary. This particularly applies to cooked foods which are to be frozen. They must be freshly prepared and cooled before freezing. Make full use of a refrigerator for this and for the temporary storage of food awaiting preparation. When preparing cooked dishes, especially those with meat and fish, always ensure good standards of hygiene. Always, for example, wash hands after handling fresh meat and fish and before touching cooked foods. Freezing is an excellent way of preserving the original, natural quality of good food, but it is also a good method of preserving bacteria!

Raw foods can frequently be bought in bulk, often at lower prices, and then prepared and cooked in bulk to save time. But rarely is it eaten in bulk. So prepare and freeze in small packages which are related in size and quantity to family portions. And don't attempt to freeze in any 24 hours a greater weight of food than that recommended by the freezer manufacturer. This maximum daily load may be heavier or lighter than the equivalent of 10% of the capacity (at the rate of 18 to 20 pounds to each cubic foot) which is sometimes suggested.

And finally, do make sure that the recommended storage times, which are for guidance only, are not grossly exceeded. Labelling each package with the name of the contents and the date of freezing will help to ensure stock rotation on the basis of 'first in—first out'.

FOODS *NOT* FOR THE FREEZER

There are a few raw and some cooked foods which do not take very kindly to home freezing. Generally speaking, they are foods with a high water content, in which case they become limp and lose their crisp texture on thawing, or the constituents separate out or they become tough and leathery. Foods not usually considered satisfactory for home freezing include:

Salad vegetables to be eaten raw, e.g. lettuce, cucumber, watercress, celery, chicory and tomatoes, though celery and tomatoes can be frozen for use in cooked dishes;

Bananas, avocados, apples, pears and whole melons to be eaten raw, though some of these can be converted into a purée, or sliced and frozen in sugar or syrup;

Whole eggs in shell, which will crack;

Sour and single cream (less than 40% butter fat), due to separation;

Milk (not homogenised), due to separation.

Some cooked or baked foods are not recommended, including:

Hard-boiled eggs

Royal icing and frostings

Custard pies and tarts

Soft meringues

Mayonnaise

Boiled potatoes

Stuffed poultry

Foods with a high proportion of gelatine.

And lastly, there are some foods which are available all the year round and are quick and easy to prepare, which may not be worth freezing simply because they take up valuable freezer space, at the expense of something really worthwhile. This list includes cabbage, root vegetables, rice, pasta and the pulses, but this is a personal preference. Excluded from the home freezing list also might be the basic commodity foods like potato chips, which can be purchased commercially frozen and stored in the freezer for up to three months.

BASIC PREPARATION
BREAD AND CAKES

Nearly all bakery products are highly perishable and become stale very quickly at normal kitchen and pantry temperatures. The crust of freshly baked bread is very dry, whilst the interior crumb is soft and moist. Even if freshly baked bread is wrapped in moisture-resistant waxed paper to retard staling, moisture in the crumb is gradually drawn into the crisp, dry crust. But home freezing freshly baked bread, immediately it has cooled in sealed polythene bags, greatly retards the movement of moisture in the bread and slows down staling and drying. This applies to bread loaves, especially sliced loaves, rolls, muffins, doughnuts, Danish pastries and cooked yeast mixtures. Loaves and bakery products can be taken from the freezer, wrapped in foil, replacing the polythene bag, put into an oven to thaw and even after several weeks storage will have a freshly-baked flavour and texture. Individual slices of bread taken from the package, which must be resealed, will thaw quickly or can be toasted without first thawing. Especially useful are bread crumbs prepared in bulk and frozen in conveniently sized polythene bags.

Uncooked doughs using yeast as a raising agent can be frozen too, but the critical factor is the short frozen-storage stability of yeast. Even after storage for a few weeks, the proving times of doughs increase quite rapidly and the yeast content should be increased to compensate for its reduced effectiveness. Better results are obtained if yeast-raised products are baked or, in the case of doughnuts, fried, before freezing.

The same principles apply to cakes, shortbread and biscuits, except that in the fresh state, they do not stale so rapidly as bread. Similarly cakes, biscuits and similar confections will retain their flavour and texture for a longer time if they are baked before freezing.

Cakes can be filled and decorated before freezing but, if a frosting or boiled icing is to be used, this should be done during thawing. Royal icing goes soft and spongy during frozen storage and only icings with a relatively high fat-content can be frozen satisfactorily, as can margarine-based cream and fudge fillings. If eggs are ingredients in a recipe, better results will be obtained if egg *yolks*, rather than whole eggs, are used. A high quality margarine, instead of butter, will usually result in a better product which is to be frozen.

It is easier to finally wrap and seal soft cakes and sponges after they have hardened in the freezer. Moisture- and vapour-proof paper laid in between layers of cake before freezing will prevent sticking if fillings are to be added during thawing. Cream sponges or similar filled cakes can be neatly cut into portions before fully thawed.

Large loaves and cakes can be wrapped and sealed in gusseted polythene bags, in moisture- and vapour-proof paper or aluminium foil. Small rolls, cakes and biscuits can be packed in rigid cartons using a sheet of moisture- and vapour-proof paper between layers. Bought, commercially-wrapped loaves should be stored in a polythene bag and sealed with paper-covered wire or similar fastener so that portions can be removed and the bag resealed quickly excluding as much air as possible.

Freezer Storage Life:

Baked bread, croissants, Danish pastry	up to 1 month
Cakes, scones and biscuits	up to 6 months
Sandwiches (excluding fillings of hard-boiled egg, tomato, cucumber, banana)	up to 2 months
Unbaked yeast dough	up to 1 month
Uncooked cake and biscuit mixtures	up to 3 months

DAIRY PRODUCTS

The most popular dairy foods—butter, cheese, eggs, cream and milk—are always available and, except for a few speciality or luxury frozen packs, there is usually little to be gained in home freezing these basic types of food which will store quite well in a refrigerator for several days.

Eggs can be prepared and frozen whole (but not in their shells) or, better still, the yolks and whites can be frozen separately. Use only clean, sound, high-quality fresh eggs and discard, for freezing purposes, those which are cracked, yolks containing blood spots and any which are off colour.

For short term storage only, whole eggs can be cracked and put into individual containers for freezing. However, for longer storage, it is best to mix the yolks and whites gently together, adding salt at the rate of $\frac{1}{2}$ teaspoon, or sugar at the rate of $\frac{1}{2}$ tablespoon, to every 6 eggs to prevent them thickening. The lightly-beaten mixture can be frozen in an ice-cube tray and the individual blocks can then be transferred to a polythene bag and sealed. Alternatively, freeze the liquid egg in 4-, 6- or 8-egg portions in a rigid container leaving headspace before sealing. Label the packs with the number of eggs and the addition of salt or sugar. Sweetened eggs can be used for cakes and puddings, salted eggs in savoury dishes. Depending upon the size of the eggs used, between 2 and 3 tablespoons of the thawed mixture will be equivalent to one egg in shell. If yolks and whites are to be frozen separately (cooling the eggs in a refrigerator will assist separation), the yolks should be stirred, but not beaten, adding a little salt or sugar. Whites need no special preparation other than a very gentle stir and the addition of a little salt or sugar. If a specially smooth texture is preferred, sieve the whites before freezing. All thawed eggs should be used immediately, whilst they are still cooler than room temperature.

Hard-boiled eggs do not freeze satisfactorily and should not be used in savoury dishes or as sandwich fillings, etc.

Milk

Whole milk is not usually preserved by home freezing, primarily because the denaturation of the milk protein during freezing is irreversible.

Pasteurised milk, which has also been homogenised, can be frozen and stored for a short time, freezing in waxed cartons and leaving a headspace before sealing.

Cream

Like whole milk, single cream will separate during freezing. Double cream, with not less than 40% butter fat and whipping cream with a little sugar (one tablespoon to each pint of cream) folded in will freeze satisfactorily, the higher the butter fat content, the better will be the result. If there is any separation during thawing, this can often be corrected by gentle stirring. Pack in wax cartons as for milk.

Butter and Cheese

These two prepared dairy products can be frozen by overwrapping the commercial packaging with polythene, moisture- and vapour-proof paper or aluminium foil and sealing. However, hard cheese may become rather crumbly after several weeks frozen storage. Cream and cottage cheeses also have a relatively short high-quality life but if grated and/or mixed with whipped cream, they make good fillings for sandwiches that are to be frozen. Grated cheese alone freezes and stores well and can be packed in small portions—enough for one serving for the family in dishes like macaroni or cauliflower cheese or to add to a white sauce, using about 3 ozs. of grated cheddar, for example, to one pint of white sauce. Grated cheese from the freezer also makes an appetising garnish to pasta dishes and soups.

Ice-Cream

Home-made ice-cream, prepared from milk, whole eggs and yolks, sugar and cream with a favourite flavour of vanilla, chocolate or strawberry can be frozen in ice trays (without the dividers) or in a shallow rigid aluminium container. To achieve a light texture, the mix must be whipped several times during the freezing time to aerate it as much as possible. Just before the mix becomes firm, the rigid container can be lined with foil after the final whipping, so that the final hardening takes place in the foil which can then be removed in a block from the rigid container, overwrapped and sealed for storage.

Commercially prepared ice-cream can be stored for up to one month in a food freezer. To reduce the possibility of shrinkage and to retain the soft aerated texture of bought ice-cream, overwrap the original package with polythene and seal.

The ideal serving temperature for ice-cream is a little higher than the storage temperature and the best texture and full flavour will be enjoyed if the quantity of ice-cream for serving is removed from the freezer and allowed to soften for a short time at room temperature or, better still, for about half an hour in a refrigerator.

Freezer Storage Life:

Eggs whole (mixed)	up to 6 months
yolks	up to 9 months
whites	up to 9 months
Milk (homogenised)	up to 3 months
Cream (high butter fat)	up to 3 months
Butter (salted)	up to 3 months
(unsalted)	up to 6 months
Cheese (soft and blue)	up to 3 months
(hard and grated)	up to 6 months
Ice-Cream (home-made)	up to 3 months
(commercial)	up to 1 month

FISH

The advantages gained by freezing fish are probably greater than for any other kind of food, mainly because fish is frequently caught a long way from the place where it is cooked and eaten. But fish deteriorates very quickly even when chilled, so only very fresh fish should be frozen—literally within hours, rather than days, of leaving the water. In practice, this eliminates the purchase of fish for home freezing from an inland fishmonger or store, and means that home freezing is limited to those who live near enough to the sea or rivers to be sure that the fish really is fresh. For others, it is preferable to buy commercially frozen fish from the retail frozen-food cabinet which, in many cases, will result in a higher quality and be more economical than home freezing after taking into

account the wastage from cleaning, gutting and trimming and the time spent in preparation. Bought frozen fish can, of course, be used as an ingredient for cooked fish dishes to be frozen at home.

The preparation of fish for home freezing depends upon the type of fish and how it is to be served, either whole or as steaks or fillets.

Whole Fish

Before freezing, round fish should be washed and the scales, gut, fins and eyes removed and the fish then thoroughly washed again in running water, drained and dried. Flat fish is similarly prepared, removing the dark skin, if preferred. If appropriate for table service, the head and tail can also be removed. Very often, the local fishmonger would undertake this initial preparation, if he is advised as to what is required and provided it can be done quickly.

To increase the high-quality storage life, whole fish can be glazed to give better protection. After initial freezing in temporary wrapping, the whole fish is dipped in ice-cold brine solution (2 ounces of salt to 1 pint of water) for about $\frac{1}{2}$ minute. A film of glaze will form over the whole fish which is then returned to the freezer to reharden. The process is repeated until a good glaze seals the entire surface of the fish. Finally seal the fish in a polythene bag or seal in aluminium foil. Large fish which have been glazed require careful handling and need some rigid support in storage to avoid cracking the glaze.

Fish Steaks and Fillets

After thorough washing and draining, prepare the fish as for cooking in steaks or fillets. Wrap in polythene sheet or bags, or in aluminium foil, excluding as much air as possible and seal with freezer tape. The quantity of fish in each package should be appropriate to meal-time requirements and separate fillets and steaks should be interleaved with two thicknesses of moisture- and vapour-proof material. This prevents the pieces of fish freezing to each other and allows individual steaks and fillets to be separated and cooked without first thawing.

Shellfish

This kind of fish especially is recommended for home freezing only if kept cool and prepared and frozen within a day of being taken from the sea.

Crab and Lobster

They should be bought alive and cooked before freezing by plunging into salted boiling water. After cooling, the meat can be removed from the shells and claws and packed into polythene or waxed cartons or aluminium foil containers, preferably separating the white from the brown meat. The large shells can be washed and oiled and kept for serving the crab and lobster at a later date. Again, local fishmongers may be prepared to cook and separate the meat from the shells.

Oysters and Scallops

These shellfish are best frozen uncooked, but they must first be removed from their shells. Wash to remove all traces of sand, then open the shells over a strainer to collect the natural juices. Wash the fish in a brine solution (1 tablespoon of salt to 1 quart of water) and pack in polythene or waxed cartons or foil containers. Cover the fish with the natural juices, leave headspace and seal the lids.

Prawns and Shrimps

It is best to freeze prawns and shrimps uncooked, as they toughen during storage after cooking. The shells of the uncooked fish can be left on, but the heads and tails should be removed. They should be thoroughly washed in cold salted water, drained and packed as for crabs and lobsters. The shells and veins can be removed during thawing.

Freezer Storage Life:

White fish cod, haddock, plaice, sole and whiting	up to 6 months
Oily fish halibut, herring, mackerel, mullet, salmon, turbot and trout	up to 3 months
Crab and lobster (cooked)	up to 3 months
Oysters and scallops (uncooked)	up to 3 months
Prawns and shrimps (uncooked)	up to 3 months
Most commercially frozen fish packs	up to 3 months

FRUIT

All fruits achieve their full flavour, desirable texture and colour when at the peak of maturity and this is the right time to harvest them for freezing. Over-ripe fruit is often too soft to handle without crushing and bruising and may result in a disappointing product after freezing. Keep fruit cool between harvesting and preparation to retain the firmness and avoid bruising.

There are several ways of preparing and freezing fruit, the method selected depending mainly upon the type of fruit and the use subsequently intended. Fruit can be frozen whole, in halves or in slices and can be frozen separately, in a dry pack, in dry sugar, in a sugar syrup or turned into a purée.

Fruits which have a relatively tough skin, gooseberries and currants, for example, need only be washed and dried and packed into polythene tubs or bags, without additional ingredients, especially if they are to be used for jam making or cooking. The addition of sugar or sugar syrup will, however, help to retain colour and flavour and also lengthen the storage life by protecting the fruit from oxidisation.

Soft fruits which normally produce a lot of juice, such as raspberries and strawberries, are normally best packed in dry sugar, especially if they are to be served as a cold dessert; otherwise a sugar syrup can be used. Other fruits containing less juice, apricots and blackberries, for example, freeze well in a sugar syrup, but, of course, can be packed in dry sugar for dessert use.

Discolouring of Fruit

The enzymes present in light-coloured fruit cause the flesh to darken very quickly after peeling and slicing. This particularly applies to apples, pears and peaches. This discoloration can be almost prevented by speedy preparation and placing pieces of fruit into a syrup solution but, even so, they may brown slightly. A more effective inhibitor is ascorbic acid (better known as Vitamin C). An ascorbic acid solution is made by dissolving 500 milligrammes of ascorbic acid in 1 pint of water, which provides a solution of average strength. Tablets of ascorbic acid can be purchased from most large chemists but may be in different tablet strengths or even in crystalline form. In the latter case, one teaspoon of crystalline ascorbic acid is equivalent to six 500 mgm. tablets. Tablets will dissolve more quickly if they are first crushed into a powder. The solution should not be made up in iron or copper containers.

If fruit to be treated with ascorbic acid is to be frozen separately or in a dry sugar pack, first dip it in the solution, then drain and dry and freeze separately or in dry sugar.

For fruit to be treated and packed in a sugar syrup, dissolve 500 mgms. of ascorbic acid in a teaspoon of cold water and add to each pint of cold sugar syrup.

Freezing Separately

This method of freezing produces free-flow packs of individual fruits and is most suitable for small whole fruits, such as raspberries, strawberries, blackberries and gooseberries. After cleaning, using water only if essential, dry the fruits and spread them out in a single layer in a polythene bag which is lying on a flat aluminium baking tray and put into the freezer. Small fruits will freeze separately in a few hours and can then be shaken gently down into a free-flow pack. Fill the pack with more fruit from other trays and seal. This method takes a little more time and takes quite a lot of space for freezing but produces separately frozen fruits which are very convenient to use. Any quantity from one or two fruits for garnishing or decoration to several portions can be taken from the pack whenever required and the pack can be resealed for continued storage. This method is, of course, equally suitable for other kinds of food—for small and diced vegetables, for example.

Freezing in Dry Sugar

After cleaning and drying, sprinkle the fruit with sugar, normally using $\frac{1}{4}$ pound of sugar to each pound of fruit, but this can be adjusted if the fruit is preferred less or more sweet. When adding sugar, work in small quantities at a time and gently shake or stir until the fruit is evenly coated with sugar. Pack into polythene bags or waxed cartons, leave headspace and seal.

Freezing in Sugar Syrup

The sugar syrup should be prepared and cooled before adding to the fruit, allowing not less than $\frac{1}{3}$ pint of syrup for each pound of fruit. Syrup solutions are normally used in one of the three following strengths:

Light sugar syrup (30%)
$8\frac{1}{2}$ ounces sugar to 1 pint water
Medium sugar syrup (40%)
13 ounces sugar to 1 pint water
Heavy sugar syrup (50%)
20 ounces sugar to 1 pint water

The proportions of sugar to water remain unchanged whatever quantity of syrup is made. Stir the sugar into the water, bring to the boil and simmer only long enough to ensure that all the sugar is dissolved. Cover the pan and allow to cool before use. When cold, add ascorbic acid solution, if appropriate. The syrup is poured over the fruit, packed in rigid polythene or waxed containers and allowed to stand for a short time whilst the syrup penetrates the fruit. Ensure that all fruit is covered, using greaseproof paper in the top of the pack if the fruit is buoyant, leave headspace and seal.

Sometimes, after low-temperature storage, a white patch might appear on fruit frozen in sugar syrup and has the appearance of mould. This is, in fact, a change taking place in the sugar which forms sucrose hydrate. It is harmless and disappears when the fruit is thawed. The substitution of a quarter of the sugar by glucose will normally overcome this problem.

Purées and Juices

Fruit which has been put aside because of blemishes, bruises or over-ripeness, can be frozen as a purée or juice for later use in sauces, cold desserts, toppings for cold sweets, for baby foods and as a breakfast drink. Apples and tomatoes should be cooked first. Fruit is simply passed through a nylon sieve and sugar can be added (at about 3 to 4 ounces to each pound of fruit) according to taste. Pour the purée or juice into a rigid container, leave headspace and seal.

Apples

Peel, core and slice. Use ascorbic acid solution to prevent browning. Blanch (see vegetable blanching) for 2 to 3 minutes for dry pack. Alternatively, pack in dry sugar or medium sugar syrup. Cook and make into purée.

Apricots

Freeze in halves or peel and slice. Always remove stone for long-period storage. Pack in a medium sugar syrup with ascorbic acid solution.

Avocados

Whole or sliced fruits do not freeze well. Best frozen as a purée, adding 1 teaspoon of lemon juice to 1 pint of purée. Season purée with salt and pepper or sweeten with sugar.

Bilberries and Blackberries

Remove stalks, wash and dry. Freeze separately in dry pack, in heavy sugar syrup or dry sugar.

Blackcurrants

Strip currants off stem, wash and dry. Freeze separately and pack dry for jam-making or juice. Alternatively, in heavy sugar syrup or dry sugar.

Cherries

Select only fully ripened fruit, remove stalks, wash well and dry. Preferably remove stones. Pack in light sugar syrup.

Citrus fruits: lemons, oranges and grapefruits etc.

Peel and remove all pith. Separate into segments and pack in medium sugar syrup. Use any juice to make up syrup for marmalade and jam-making. Alternatively, wash, dry and freeze whole.

Cranberries

Remove stalks, wash and dry. Freeze whole in dry sugar for sauce-making. Alternatively, sieve for purée and add sugar to taste.

Damsons

Wash, halve and remove stones. Pack dry or in dry sugar for jam-making. Pack in heavy sugar syrup with ascorbic acid solution for use as dessert. Alternatively, sieve and freeze as a purée.

Gooseberries

Top and tail, wash and dry. Pack dry for jam-making or freeze separately, sprinkled with sugar for cooking. Pack large dessert varieties in heavy sugar syrup.

Grapes

Seedless varieties can be frozen separately whole, otherwise, halve and remove seeds. Pack in light sugar syrup.

Greengages

Wash and dry, halve and remove stones. Pack in heavy sugar syrup with ascorbic acid solution.

Loganberries

Remove stalks, wash and dry and pack dry or in dry sugar.

Melon

Cantaloup and honeydew melons lose their crisp texture after freezing, so the best method is to halve the fruit, remove all seeds and scoop out the flesh in melon balls or cut in cubes. Place pieces immediately in a light sugar syrup. Alternatively, sprinkle the pieces with lemon juice and pack in dry sugar.

Nectarines and Peaches

Avoid handling as much as possible. Skin, halve, remove stones and cut into slices, if preferred. Avoid discolouring by preparing quickly and plunging into medium sugar syrup with double strength ascorbic acid solution (1000 mgms. ascorbic acid to 1 pint of cold sugar syrup). If a dry sugar pack is preferred, dip prepared fruit into ascorbic acid solution before sprinkling with dry sugar.

Pears

Do not freeze very well. Best as a purée. Otherwise, wash, peel, core and quarter or slice. Immediately sprinkle with lemon juice. Immerse in light sugar syrup and simmer 1 to 2 minutes. Drain the fruit, cool and pack in fresh medium sugar syrup with ascorbic acid solution.

Pineapple

Wash and dry, peel and core. Cut into slices or cubes. Pack in a light sugar syrup using any pineapple juice from preparation. Alternatively, crushed pineapple pieces can be frozen in a dry sugar pack.

Plums

Wash and dry, halve and remove stones. Pack dry or with dry sugar for jam-making. Alternatively, pack in heavy sugar syrup with ascorbic acid solution.

Raspberries

Avoid washing if home-grown without insecticide spray. Freeze separately or in dry sugar.

Redcurrants

Strip currants off stem, wash and dry. Freeze separately and pack dry for jam-making. Alternatively, in dry sugar or in heavy sugar syrup.

Rhubarb

Select young and tender stalks. Wash and dry and cut into 1-inch pieces. Best results if lightly cooked, then drain and pack in dry sugar for pies and preserves or in heavy sugar syrup for dessert use. (Use heavy sugar syrup for light cooking and cool before packing.)

Strawberries

Remove hulls, avoid washing if home-grown without insecticide spray. Freeze whole fruit separately sprinkled with dry sugar. Alternatively, whole or sliced in dry sugar pack.

Tomatoes

Satisfactory only if later to be used for cooking. For this purpose, select small, firm whole tomatoes, wash and dry and freeze separately, some may burst during freezing. Normally more satisfactory if frozen after sieving as a purée.

Note: when packing fruit purée and juices in rigid containers, leave $\frac{1}{2}$ inch to $\frac{3}{4}$ inch headspace to allow for expansion during freezing.

Freezer Storage Life:

Most fruits will store satisfactorily for 9 to 12 months when packed in dry sugar or in sugar syrup. If packed dry, up to 6 months. Avocados have a relatively short storage life of up to 2 months and pineapple up to 3 months. Purées should be stored for not longer than 6 months—juices up to 4 months.

MEAT

The object of making significant financial savings by buying carcase meat and freezing at home for later consumption is rarely accomplished. In the first place, a very large freezer would be required to freeze and store the various cuts of meat but, more important, the degree of skill required for maturing and then butchering into family size joints and individual cuts is rarely available. In practice, a professional high-quality butcher will be the main source of supply of joints and cuts of beef, lamb, pork and veal, ready for final trimming, packaging and freezing at home.

With all types of meat, trim off excess fat and remove, or have removed, bones as far as practicable to save freezer space and simplify packaging. Bones which have been cut out can be used to make stock which, after cooling, should be skimmed of fat and frozen in conveniently sized containers (such as an ice-cube tray).

Airtight packaging of meat, with the packaging fitting snugly and tightly to the meat, is especially important to prevent dehydration, freezer burn and rancidity.

Large Joints

Any projecting bones or ribs should first be protected with clean fresh muslin or greaseproof paper before overwrapping in foil or sealing in a gusseted polythene bag. Exclude as much air as possible. The thinner the package, the faster it will freeze and thaw.

Small Cuts

Chops and steaks are best interleaved with two sheets of moisture- and vapour-proof paper before being overwrapped to make packages of an appropriate number of portions. This also permits individual chops and steaks to be taken from the package which is then resealed; individual pieces of meat can be cooked without first thawing.

Cooking

Meat can be cooked whilst still frozen and this is the best way to cook chops, steaks, diced meat and other small pieces of meat. However, for more even cooking, large joints and cuts should be at least partially thawed, ideally in a refrigerator. Small joints may take only a few hours to thaw but larger joints of 4 and 5 pounds weight will need to be left overnight in a refrigerator to thaw through, depending upon the thickness of the joint. It is advisable not to leave home-frozen meat too long in the thawed state, to prevent the loss of natural juices by 'drip'.

Refreezing

As in the case of fish, fruit, poultry and vegetables, home-frozen and commercially-frozen meat can be used to make up special dishes and then refrozen. But it is important that the meat is cooked before refreezing. The storage life is then not so long, of course, as the equivalent uncooked raw meat.

Minced Meat, Offal and Sausages

These meat products should be frozen only if they are absolutely fresh. Even then, with careful packaging, the storage life is short. Sausages should be interleaved with moisture- and vapour-proof material before overwrapping, to ease separation for cooking.

Stews and Casseroles

The only two points to remember when preparing cooked stews and casseroles for freezing are to skim excess fat from the surface after cooling and not to add the full quantity of normal seasoning. Freeze in foil-lined rigid dishes and remove from the container, overwrap and seal for storage.

Freezer Storage Life:

The storage life of meat depends upon, amongst other factors, the quality and freshness of the meat at the time of freezing, the percentage of fat and, in the case of sausages, minced meat and cured meats, on the amount of seasoning. Assuming again a steady storage temperature not warmer than $-18°C$ ($0°F$), the following is a general guide to the storage life of meat:

Beef	up to 9 months
Lamb	up to 9 months
Pork	up to 4 months
Veal	up to 4 months
Offal	up to 2 months
Minced meat and sausages (freshly made)	
	up to 1 month
Cured meats	up to 1 month
Cooked stews and casseroles	up to 2 months

PASTRIES

All pastries freeze well but cooked pastries do not store quite so long as uncooked. Longer storage times are achieved if margarine rather than butter is used as an ingredient. Flaky, puff and short-crust pastry can be made from the usual recipes and portioned into thin slabs which will freeze and thaw fairly quickly, ready for rolling and shaping. It is even more convenient to roll and shape the pastry before freezing, so that it can go straight into the oven from the freezer for baking. Foil pie-dishes can be lined with pastry and the base pricked over with a fork before freezing. Shaped pastry of course needs very careful packaging and then handling after freezing to avoid breaking the fragile shells. Baked short-crust and flaky pastry pie- and flan-shells are useful standby items in the freezer as they only require a short reheating time to be made ready for fillings and made into dishes which would otherwise require a lengthy preparation time. Cooked puff pastry rather wastes freezer space and is especially fragile.

Freezer Storage Life:

Uncooked short-crust, flaky and puff pastry	
	up to 9 months
Cooked pastry cases (using margarine and shortening)	
	up to 6 months
Puff pastry made with butter	up to 3 months

POULTRY AND GAME

The increasing cost of high-quality meat and at the same time the wider availability of quick-frozen poultry has increased the popularity and usage of poultry which can be successfully home-frozen too, for use in a great variety of nourishing and tasty dishes. Game, which at one time was available only when in season, can now be served for many more months in the year. However, it's not worth freezing any other than young plump and fresh birds and it's wise to reject game which has been badly shot.

Poultry

After plucking, poultry should be hung in a cool place for twenty-four hours before drawing and cleaning. Birds can then be frozen whole or in joints depending upon how they are to be cocked and used. If giblets are needed, they must be washed, dried and packed separately, because the storage life is much shorter than for the eviscerated bird. The stuffing of poultry before freezing is definitely not recommended, as this not only significantly slows down the speed of freezing and thawing but may cause 'off' flavours to develop during frozen storage.

Whole birds should be trussed as for normal cooking and any projecting bones protected with muslin or several thicknesses of greaseproof paper. Each whole bird can then be inserted into a heavy-gauge gusseted polythene bag and sealed only after as much air as possible has been drawn out. Lowering the loaded bag into cold water will help push out the air.

Joints and quarters can be wrapped individually or several pieces packed in bags or containers, in the latter case separating each piece from the other with a double thickness of moisture- and vapour-proof paper. When packing joints and quarters of chicken, bear in mind that this would be a good time to make chicken stock from the carcase. After the stock has cooled, skim off excess fat and freeze in ice-cube trays before wrapping and sealing. Turkey and duck especially are likely to develop rancidity after long storage, so when jointing and quartering remove as much fat as possible.

Game Birds

The preparation of game is similar to that for poultry, except that the hanging period is usually very much longer, depending upon the taste preferred. Game birds should not be hung after freezing. Water birds should be plucked, drawn, washed and cleaned as soon as possible after shooting to prevent contamination of the flesh by any fish content in the intestine. Pack game birds whole and individually in heavy-gauge gusseted polythene bags, protecting bones and excluding as much air as possible.

Rabbit and hare should be skinned, cleaned, washed and then portioned before freezing as they are normally cooked in joints and pieces.

It is very important that large whole poultry and game should be thawed right through before cooking, preferably in a refrigerator. Turkeys over 20 pounds in weight will probably take three days or so to thaw and average weight chickens up to twenty-four hours. But small joints, quarters and pieces of poultry and game, can be cooked or used as ingredients for special recipes without first thawing, ensuring that they are eventually cooked right through to the centre.

Freezer Storage Life:

Chicken (without giblets)	9 to 12 months
Giblets	up to 3 months
Duck	up to 6 months
Goose	up to 6 months
Turkey	up to 6 months
Game birds	up to 6 months
Hare and rabbit	up to 6 months

VEGETABLES

Nearly all vegetables which can be preserved by freezing compare very favourably, from a nutritional and from a quality point of view, with genuinely fresh produce. And if young, tender, not over-mature vegetables are correctly prepared and packaged, they can be stored in the freezer from one season almost to the next. Nearly all vegetables freeze successfully, but—naturally—some better than others. Those with a high water content and salad vegetables become limp and lose their crispness, which cannot be restored on thawing. Tomatoes and onions can be frozen raw but are then really only suitable as ingredients for sauces, soups and casseroles. Generally, those vegetables which are normally cooked before eating are the ones which freeze best, especially if prepared and frozen within a few hours of harvesting.

To prepare for home freezing, vegetables should be podded, peeled, sliced and washed as for normal cooking. But they must then be blanched (scalded) for a few minutes to inactivate enzymes and stop the development of 'off' flavours during long storage. Blanching is also essential to preserve colour, flavour and texture. The only possible exceptions from the need for blanching are the vegetables with a strong natural flavour or low enzymatic activity including onions, peppers and parsley, for short storage life only.

Blanching vegetables

Blanching is most easily done by immersing the vegetables held in a wire basket in a large pan of briskly boiling water. Process small quantities at a time, say 1 pound of vegetables to 6 pints of water. The blanching time begins when the water returns to boiling after the immersion of the vegetables. The scalding process should be stopped at the end of the blanching time by plunging the vegetables in ice-cold water, to cool as quickly as possible. All that remains is to drain and dry the produce as much as possible and pack for freezing. The usual method of packing is in conveniently sized polythene bags or cartons, to hold 4, 8 or 16 ounces, but many vegetables and mixtures of sliced vegetables can be frozen separately to produce a convenient free-flow pack, as described in the fruit section.

Artichokes (globe)
Remove coarse outer leaves and stalks, trim tops and stems. Add lemon juice to blanching water. Blanch a few at a time for 7 minutes. Chill, drain and dry. Pack and seal in rigid containers.

Asparagus
Wash and scrape stalks and trim to approximately equal lengths. Divide into convenient portions of thin, medium and thick stalks. Blanch for 2, 3 or 4 minutes respectively. Cool, drain and dry. Pack tips to stalks in rigid containers. Large bundles in one container can be separated with two sheets of greaseproof paper.

Aubergines
Wash thoroughly and cut into $\frac{1}{2}$-inch slices with stainless steel knife. Blanch for 4 minutes. Chill, drain and dry. Pack in layers in rigid container separated by two sheets of greaseproof paper.

Beans (broad) Pick the pods before fully mature. Shell and blanch beans for 3 minutes. Cool, drain, dry and pack.

Beans (French and runner)
Select young tender beans which snap cleanly. Wash and trim ends. Leave whole or slice thickly. Blanch whole French beans for 3 minutes; if sliced, only 2 minutes. Blanch whole runner beans for 2 minutes or, if sliced, 1 minute. Cool, drain, dry and pack.

Beetroot
Best to freeze young and small beets. Leave whole and cook until tender. Rub off skins. Pack in rigid containers. If large beets are used, they should be sliced or diced before cooking.

Broccoli
Trim stalks, cut out any woody parts, and trim stalks to approximately equal length. Divide into thin, medium and thick stems and blanch for 3, 4 or 5 minutes respectively. Pack sprig-to-stalk in layers separated by two sheets of greaseproof paper in rigid containers.

Brussels spouts
Trim, remove discoloured leaves and cross cut the stalks. Wash thoroughly, blanch 3 to 5 minutes, depending on size. Drain and dry and pack in containers or polythene bags. Can be frozen separately.

Cabbage (and spring greens)
If considered worthwhile freezing, select crisp, tender cabbage. Trim off outer discoloured leaves, wash thoroughly in salted water and cut or tear in shreds. Blanch for 2 minutes, chill and drain as much as possible. Pack in portions in polythene bags and seal.

Carrots
Remove tops, wash and scrape. Leave small young carrots whole, slice or dice larger carrots. Blanch whole carrots 5 minutes, sliced or diced carrots 3 minutes. Chill, drain, dry and pack. Small whole carrots can be frozen separately.

Cauliflower
Choose white firm heads. Remove outer leaves and separate into sprigs. Soak in cold water, then blanch for 3 minutes (4 minutes for larger sprigs). Add lemon juice to blanching water. Cool, drain, dry and pack in rigid container.

Celeriac
Wash, trim and scrape, cut into slices. Blanch for 6 to 8 minutes. Chill, drain, dry and pack in polythene bags.

Celery

Suitable only for later use as a cooked vegetable or as ingredient for cooked dishes. Remove coarse outer stalks and strings. Wash and cut into 2- to 3-inch lengths. Blanch for 3 to 4 minutes depending on size or up to 8 minutes for celery hearts. Cool, drain and dry. Freeze celery pieces separately if to be used for flavouring. Pack in polythene bags or waxed cartons.

Corn on the cob

Choose firm and young kernels, not over-mature. Remove outer husks, trim ends and wash. Blanch for 5 to 8 minutes depending on size. Freeze separately and then pack in polythene bags or waxed cartons. Do not overcook when reheating.

Courgettes

Wash and cut into 1-inch slices. Blanch for 3 minutes. Cool, drain, dry and pack in rigid container, interleaving layers with 2 sheets of greaseproof paper.

Leeks

Remove coarse outer leaves and trim ends. Slice and wash well in running water. Blanch 2 to 4 minutes depending on size. Cool, drain and dry. Pack in rigid container or polythene bag. Can be cooked in white sauce and frozen in rigid containers in family-size portions.

Mushrooms

Wash and peel field mushrooms. Wash and trim stems of cultivated mushrooms. Drain and dry as much as possible. Slice mushrooms over 1 inch across. Put into cold water with lemon juice to prevent discoloration. Blanching not essential, but can be sautéed in margarine, providing all excess fat is drained off before packing in rigid containers.

Onions

Suitable only for later use as cooked vegetable and as flavouring ingredient. Peel and slice. Blanch for 2 minutes. Pack in small quantities in polythene bags or waxed cartons. Seal well to prevent cross-flavouring in freezer. These also freeze well in white sauce.

Parsnips

Choose young small parsnips. Scrape and wash. Cut into quarters or slices. Blanch for 2 minutes, cool, drain, dry and pack in polythene bags or waxed cartons.

Peas

Use only young sweet peas. Pod and discard any discoloured peas. Blanch in small quantities for $1\frac{1}{2}$ minutes. Cool, drain and pack in portions in polythene bags or waxed cartons.

Peppers (red and green)

Wash, remove seeds and halve or slice. Remove only top to scrape out seeds if later to be stuffed. Blanch for 2 minutes and freeze separately after cooling and drying or pack in slices or halves in waxed cartons or polythene bags.

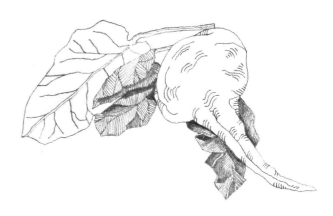

Spinach

Use young tender leaves. Wash well in running water. Blanch for 2 minutes and press out all excess water. Dry as much as possible and pack in rigid container or polythene bag in portion quantities.

Turnips and Swedes

Remove thick peel and cut into 1-inch cubes. Blanch for 3 minutes and cool, drain, dry and pack in polythene bags or waxed cartons.

Freezer Storage Life:

Most vegetables	from 9 to 12 months
Beetroot	up to 6 months
Carrots	up to 8 months
Cauliflower	up to 8 months
Leeks	up to 6 months
Onions	up to 3 months
Herbs (unblanched)	up to 3 months

OVEN TEMPERATURE CHART

Table of temperature equivalents for oven thermostat markings with divisions to indicate approximate description and gas marks

DESCRIPTION	°FAHRENHEIT	GAS MARK	°CELSIUS (CENTIGRADE)
COOL	150°F 175°F 200°F 225°F	$\frac{1}{4}$–2	70°C 80°C 100°C 110°C
SLOW	250°F 275°F 300°F 325°F	2–3	130°C 140°C 150°C 170°C
MODERATE	350°F	4	180°C
MODERATELY HOT	375°F 400°F	5 6	190°C 200°C
HOT	425°F	7	220°C
VERY HOT	450°F 475°F 500°F 525°F 550°F	8–9	230°C 240°C 250°C 270°C 290°C

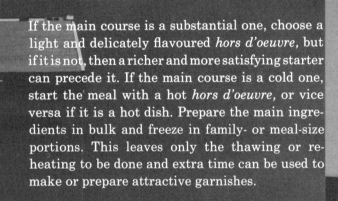

If the main course is a substantial one, choose a light and delicately flavoured *hors d'oeuvre*, but if it is not, then a richer and more satisfying starter can precede it. If the main course is a cold one, start the meal with a hot *hors d'oeuvre,* or vice versa if it is a hot dish. Prepare the main ingredients in bulk and freeze in family- or meal-size portions. This leaves only the thawing or re-heating to be done and extra time can be used to make or prepare attractive garnishes.

Hors d'Oeuvre

Avocado and Crab Cocktail
Chicken Liver Pâté
Melon and Orange Cocktail

Avocado and Crab Cocktail

2 avocado pears
2 tablespoons oil
1 tablespoon lemon juice
2 tablespoons double cream
salt and pepper

To serve:
8-ounce carton frozen crab (thawed)
paprika
Freezer Storage Life: up to 2 months

Preparation for freezing:
Halve the avocados, remove stones, and scoop the flesh into a basin. Mash with a fork and slowly add the oil and lemon juice and beat until smooth. Stir in the cream and season to taste.
Spoon into a container, cover and freeze.

To serve:
Allow to thaw out and if necessary beat again. Serve in individual glasses with chopped crab on the top. Sprinkle with a little paprika.
Serves 4

Chicken and Pork Terrine

3-pound oven-ready chicken
½-pound pork fillet
1 small onion (chopped)
1-2 cloves garlic (crushed)
2-ounce butter
salt and pepper
4 tablespoons brandy
¼ pint chicken stock
2 bay leaves

Freezer Storage Life: up to 1 month

Preparation for freezing:
Remove flesh from the chicken and chop finely or mince. Mince pork. Fry the onion and garlic in butter until transparent then mix with the chicken and pork (adding the butter as well). Add the remaining ingredients, except the bay leaves and mix well.
Grease a 2-pint terrine dish or oven-proof casserole and place the bay leaves on the base. Spoon the chicken mixture into the dish, cover with foil. Place dish in a roasting-pan with water and bake at 325°F/Gas 3 for 1–1½ hours. Leave to cool. Turn out of the dish, wrap and freeze.

To serve:
Leave to thaw overnight in the refrigerator. Remove wrapping and return to the terrine for serving.
Serves 8

Chicken Liver Pâté

1-pound chicken liver
4-ounce butter
1 onion (chopped)
salt and pepper
1 teaspoon dry mustard
2 tablespoons brandy
melted butter

To serve:
plain or melba toast
Freezer Storage Life: up to 1 month

Preparation for freezing:
Chop liver into small pieces and fry in the butter until cooked. Drain and place in a basin. Fry the onion until soft and mix with the liver adding the butter as well. If a smooth pâté is preferred put the liver and onion through a mincer or electric blender. Mix with the salt and pepper, to taste, mustard and brandy. Pack into a carton and cover the top with a little melted butter. Cover and freeze.

To serve:
Allow to thaw out either overnight in the refrigerator or 4–5 hours at room temperature. Turn out and decorate as desired or serve sliced on individual plates with plain or melba toast.
Serves 6

Smoked Trout Pâté

2 smoked trout
juice ½ lemon
¼ teaspoon cayenne pepper
ground black pepper
2-ounce cream cheese
2 teaspoons parsley (chopped)

To serve:
fingers of toast
Freezer Storage Life: up to 1 month

Preparation for freezing:
Remove skin from the trout and flake the fish into a basin. Add lemon juice, cayenne and black pepper, to taste. Mash with a wooden spoon or blend until quite smooth. Stir in the cream cheese and parsley and mix until blended.
Spoon into a container, cover and freeze.

To serve:
Allow to thaw either overnight in the refrigerator or 4–5 hours at room temperature.
Serve with fingers of brown toast.
Serves 4

Pâté de Foie

1-pound lamb's liver
2-ounce pork fat
1 tablespoon oil
1 small onion (chopped)
2-ounce mushrooms (sliced)
4-ounce pork sausage-meat
6 tablespoons white breadcrumbs
1 tablespoon almonds (chopped)
2 egg yolks
⅛ pint dry white wine
salt and pepper
3 rashers bacon

To serve:
gherkins and tomato (sliced)
Freezer Storage Life: up to 1 month

Preparation for freezing:
Cut the liver and pork fat into pieces. Heat oil in a frying-pan and fry the liver until brown. Add the pork fat and fry for a further 2 minutes. Remove liver and pork fat, mix in the onion and put through a mincer. Mix meat and onion with remaining ingredients, except the bacon rashers. Grease a 2-pound loaf-tin and place the de-rinded bacon in the base. Spoon the pâté into the tin and cover with foil. Place the tin in a roasting-pan with water (about an inch deep) and bake at 325°F/Gas 3 for 1–1½ hours. Leave to cool. Turn pâté out of the tin then wrap and freeze.

To serve:
Allow to thaw out overnight in the refrigerator. Serve sliced and garnish with sliced gherkins and tomato.
Serves 8

Melon and Orange Cocktail

1 melon
3 oranges
1 tablespoon lemon juice
caster sugar to taste

To serve:
2 tablespoons Cointreau
orange rind (optional)
Freezer Storage Life: up to 6 months

Preparation for freezing:
Halve the melon and remove the seeds. Scoop out small pieces of the fruit either with a teaspoon or melon scoop. Remove peel and pith from the oranges and divide the fruit into segments. Mix melon and oranges together, stir in the lemon juice and sugar to taste. Pack, seal and freeze.

To serve:
Let fruit thaw overnight in refrigerator, spoon into serving glasses and sprinkle each with a little Cointreau. If liked decorate with a thin whirl of orange rind.
Serves 6

Smoked Trout Pâté

Cannelloni

8-ounce cannelloni
Stuffing:
4-ounce white breadcrumbs
little milk
8-12-ounce lean bacon (finely chopped)
2 tablespoons parsley (chopped)
salt and pepper
1 egg (beaten)
1 tin tomato soup
4-6-ounce cheese (grated)

Freezer Storage Life: up to 2 months

Preparation for freezing:
Cook cannelloni in fast boiling salted water for
15 minutes and drain. Soak breadcrumbs in milk.
Fry bacon lightly for 5 minutes. Mix breadcrumbs,
bacon, parsley and seasoning and bind with egg.
Stuff cannelloni with mixture. Place in oven-proof
dish or individual foil containers, cover with soup
and sprinkle grated cheese over top. Cover with
freezer foil and seal.

To serve:
Leave to thaw slightly. Bake at 350°F/Gas 4 for
40–50 minutes or until cooked through. Brown
under the grill if necessary.
Serves 4

Ham and Mushroom Bouchées

½-pound mushrooms (sliced)
1-ounce butter
¼-pound cooked ham (diced)
½ pint Béchamel sauce (see page 57)

To serve:
1 packet frozen vol-au-vent cases or 12 pre-baked ones
parsley (chopped)
Freezer Storage Life: up to 2 months

Preparation for freezing:
Fry the mushrooms in butter until soft, drain and
mix with the ham and sauce. Add extra seasoning
if liked. Pack, seal and freeze.

To serve:
Bake frozen vol-au-vent cases according to the
instructions on the packet, or heat the pre-baked
ones. Turn the filling into a saucepan and cook
over low heat, stirring frequently, until hot. Fill
the cases with the mixture and sprinkle with
chopped parsley.
Serves 6

Fish Quenelles

1½-pound white fish (cod, haddock, etc.)
4-ounce butter (softened)
2-ounce white breadcrumbs
1 tablespoon chopped parsley
1 teaspoon grated lemon rind
3 eggs
salt
½ teaspoon cayenne pepper

To serve:
little white wine (optional)
Hollandaise sauce (p. 56)
Freezer Storage Life: up to 3 months

Preparation for freezing:
Poach the fish in a little water until cooked, drain well and remove any skin and bones. Flake the fish into a basin and beat in the butter. Add the remaining ingredients and beat until smooth. Form the mixture into small balls. Pack and freeze.

To serve:
Poach the quenelles in boiling salted water (a little white wine may be added for extra flavour) for 20 minutes. Drain well and serve with Hollandaise sauce (page 56).
Serves 6

Avocado Mousse

2 avocado pears
juice 1 lemon
3 tablespoons oil
¼ pint double cream
pinch sugar
salt and pepper

To serve:
parsley (chopped)
Freezer Storage Life: up to 2 months

Preparation for freezing:
Halve the pears, remove the stones and scoop the fruit into a basin. Mash with a fork and beat in the lemon juice. Add the oil and cream gradually, beating well until smooth. Add sugar, salt and pepper, to taste. (N.B. This can be done in an electric blender.) Spoon the mousse into a large container or into individual ones. Cover, seal and freeze.

To serve:
Allow to thaw out for 4–5 hours, spoon out into serving glasses and garnish with chopped parsley.

For **Prawn and Avocado Mousse**
Stir 2 ounces peeled prawns into the thawed mousse and garnish with a piece of lemon.
Serves 4

Taramasalata

3 slices white bread
½-pound cod roe (skinned)
1 small onion (chopped)
1 clove garlic (crushed)
juice 1 lemon
ground black pepper
4-5 tablespoons olive oil

To serve:
slices of lemon
toast
Freezer Storage Life: up to 1 month

Preparation for freezing:
Remove crusts from the bread, sprinkle the bread with cold water to make it quite damp. Mix the bread with remaining ingredients (add the oil gradually to make a soft consistency) and put through an electric blender for a few minutes until smooth. Pack, seal and freeze.

To serve:
Allow to thaw out either overnight in the refrigerator or 4–5 hours at kitchen temperature.
Spoon into individual pots or on to small plates. Serve garnished with a slice of lemon and serve toast separately.
Serves 6

There are two main types of soup—clear and thick—and like *hors d'oeuvre* the type and flavour chosen should be in harmony with, and complementary to, the main dish. Almost all soups and stocks freeze very well, providing cream, egg yolks or potatoes are added just before serving. Soups and stocks should be skimmed of all fat before freezing. If home-made stock is prepared, pour the cooled stock into ice trays and, when frozen, remove them and pack the cubes in polythene bags. A selection of meat, poultry or fish stocks provide the basis of a variety of soups and sauces. If home-made stock isn't available, then stock cubes may be substituted, but take care with the seasoning as cubes are more highly seasoned. When packing soups, ensure that there is at least $\frac{1}{4}$–$\frac{1}{2}$ inch headspace left between the top of the soup and the cover of the container (to allow for expansion during freezing).

Soups

French Onion Soup
Chilled Cucumber and Mint Soup
Tomato and Mixed Vegetable Soup
Rich Kidney Soup

Chilled Cucumber and Mint Soup

1 small onion (chopped)
2 cucumbers (peel removed and sliced)
1-ounce butter
1 pint chicken stock
2 tablespoons fresh mint (chopped) or 1 tablespoon dried
¼ pint milk
salt and pepper

To serve:
5-ounce carton yoghourt
mint or parsley (chopped)
Freezer Storage Life: up to 4 months

Preparation for freezing:
Sauté onion and cucumber in butter for 2-3 minutes. Add stock, mint, milk, salt and pepper, bring to the boil then simmer for 15 minutes. Put soup through a sieve or electric blender, leave to cool and remove any fat from the surface. Pour into containers, cover and seal. Place in the freezer.

To serve:
Remove from freezer 4–6 hours before required or leave to thaw in refrigerator overnight. Turn into a basin and lightly beat in the yoghourt. Serve garnished with sprigs of mint or chopped parsley.
Serves 4

Lentil Soup

½-pound lentils
1 onion (peeled and chopped)
1 carrot (scraped and sliced)
1 potato (peeled and sliced)
2 rashers bacon (de-rinded and chopped)
2 pints water
salt and pepper
pinch sugar

To serve:
parsley (chopped)
croûtons of fried bread
Freezer Storage Life: up to 3 months

Preparation for freezing:
Wash the lentils in cold water. Place the onion, carrot, potato and bacon in a saucepan and cook for a few minutes. Add the lentils, water, salt, pepper and sugar. Bring to the boil, then cover and simmer the soup for 1–1½ hours until the lentils are soft. Sieve the soup and when cold, pack and freeze.

To serve:
Place the soup in a saucepan and cook over low heat until thawed, bring to the boil for 3 minutes. Serve sprinkled with parsley and serve croûtons of fried bread separately.
Serves 6

Cream of Tomato Soup

2-pound tomatoes
1 onion (peeled and chopped)
1 stick celery (chopped)
1-ounce butter
2 tablespoons tomato purée
2 pints stock
1 teaspoon sugar
salt and pepper
1 tablespoon cornflour
¼ pint milk

To serve:
¼ pint cream
Freezer Storage Life: up to 3 months

Preparation for freezing:
Quarter the tomatoes and place in a large saucepan, add onion, celery and butter. Cook over low heat until the tomatoes are soft. Add purée, stock, sugar and salt and pepper. Bring to the boil, cover, then simmer the soup for 1 hour. Put the soup through a sieve and return to a clean pan. Blend cornflour with the milk and stir into the soup. Bring to the boil stirring all the time. Allow to cool, remove any excess fat, pack and freeze.

To serve:
Place the soup in a saucepan and cook over a low heat until thawed, boil for about 3 minutes. The cream can be mixed through the soup or spooned on top when served.
Serves 6

Rich Kidney Soup

¾-pound lamb's kidney (trimmed and finely chopped)
2 tablespoons seasoned flour
1-ounce cooking fat
1 onion (finely chopped)
1 teaspoon mixed herbs
salt and pepper
1 pint beef stock
½ pint red wine

Freezer Storage Life: up to 3 months

Preparation for freezing:
Coat the kidney in seasoned flour, then sauté in fat until brown. Add onions, mixed herbs, salt and pepper, stock and wine. Bring to the boil, and simmer for about ¾ hour until kidney is soft. If liked, the soup may be puréed in a blender. Cool and remove any fat. Pack and freeze.

To serve:
Bring soup to the boil, and simmer for a few minutes.
Serves 4

Cock-a-Leekie

6 leeks (washed and sliced)
1-ounce butter
2 carrots (scraped and diced)
1½ pints chicken stock
1-ounce barley
salt and pepper

To serve:
1 tablespoon chopped parsley
Freezer Storage Life: up to 4 months

Preparation for freezing:
Sauté leeks in butter, add carrots and pour in the stock. Add barley, salt and pepper. Bring to the boil, then simmer for 1 hour. Cool, remove any fat from the surface, pack and freeze.

To serve:
Turn block into a saucepan, place over low heat and when thawed add parsley and bring to the boil.
Serves 4

Artichoke Soup

2 onions (peeled and chopped)
1 stick celery (sliced)
1-ounce butter or margarine
1-pound Jerusalem artichokes (peeled and sliced)
1 pint chicken stock
½ pint milk
salt and pepper

To serve:
juice 1 lemon
¼ pint cream
parsley (chopped)
Freezer Storage Life: up to 4 months

Preparation for freezing:
Sauté onions and celery in butter or margarine for a few minutes, add artichokes, stock, milk, salt and pepper. Bring to the boil, then cover and simmer for 30 minutes until vegetables are soft. Put through a sieve or electric blender. When cool pack and freeze.

To serve:
Bring soup slowly to the boil, add lemon juice and cream. Sprinkle with chopped parsley.
Serves 4-6

Watercress Soup

1 onion (chopped)
1-ounce butter
3 bunches watercress (washed and trimmed)
1-ounce flour
1½ pints chicken stock
salt and pepper
pinch nutmeg

To serve:
cream
Freezer Storage Life: up to 4 months

Preparation for freezing:
Sauté onion in butter, add watercress, and cook
for a few minutes. Stir in the flour, stock, salt and
pepper and nutmeg. Cook for 10 minutes, then
sieve or put through an electric blender, and leave
to cool. Remove any excess fat, pack and freeze.

To serve:
Cold:—allow to thaw then stir in the cream.
Hot:—bring to the boil, pour into serving dishes
and serve with a spoonful of cream on each.
Serves 4

Celery and Pea Soup

1 head celery (prepared and sliced)
1-ounce butter or margarine
1½ pints stock
salt and pepper
8-ounce packet peas

Freezer Storage Life: up to 4 months

Preparation for freezing:
Sauté celery in butter then add stock, salt and
pepper. Bring to the boil, then simmer until celery
is tender. Add peas and cook for a further 15
minutes. This soup can be sieved or blended or if
preferred the vegetables left whole. Cool, remove
any fat from the surface, pack and freeze.

To serve:
Bring soup to the boil, simmer for a few minutes.
Serve.
Serves 4

Above, also shows Asparagus Cream Soup,
recipe see opposite

Bortsch

2 carrots (scraped and sliced)
3 sticks celery (sliced)
2 leeks (sliced)
¼-pound white cabbage (shredded)
1 onion (peeled and chopped)
1 clove garlic (crushed)
1 bay leaf
pinch thyme
3 sprigs parsley
2 pints stock
salt and pepper
pinch sugar
1 pound beetroot (shredded)
juice 1 lemon

To serve:
soured cream
Freezer Storage Life: up to 3 months

Preparation for freezing:
Place all vegetables except the beetroot into a
saucepan, pour in the stock and add salt, pepper
and sugar. Bring to the boil and simmer for 1 hour.
Put the vegetables and stock through a strainer,
or electric blender, and return to the saucepan.
Stir in the beetroot and lemon juice, bring to the
boil and simmer for ½ hour. Cool, pack and freeze.

To serve:
Place the soup in a saucepan and stir over low

heat until thawed, then boil for 3 minutes.
Serve with a spoonful of soured cream on top of
each portion.
Serves 6

Asparagus Cream Soup

1-ounce butter
1 onion (finely chopped)
1-pound asparagus or 2–8-ounce packets (frozen)
1 pint stock
pinch of nutmeg
salt and pepper
½-ounce cornflour
¼ pint milk

To serve:
⅛ pint cream
croûtons of fried bread
Freezer Storage Life: up to 4 months

Preparation for freezing:
Melt the butter in a saucepan and sauté the onion
until transparent. Scrape, trim and slice the
asparagus and add to the pan (if using frozen add
straight from the pack). Pour the stock into the
pan and add nutmeg, salt and pepper. Bring to the
boil, then simmer until asparagus is tender. Put
soup through a sieve or electric blender, return to
the pan and thicken with blended cornflour and
milk. Bring to the boil and cook for 5 minutes.
Cool quickly and remove any fat from the surface.
Pour into containers and seal. Place in the freezer.

To serve:
Turn the soup into a saucepan, place over low heat;
when thawed bring to the boil for a few minutes.
Remove from the heat and stir in the cream.
Serve garnished with croûtons of fried bread.
Serves 4

Cream of Chicken Soup with Tarragon

1 onion (chopped)
1-ounce butter
1-ounce flour
1½ pints chicken stock
1 teaspoon fresh or ½ teaspoon dried tarragon

To serve:
1 egg yolk
¼ pint single cream
Freezer Storage Life: up to 4 months

Preparation for freezing:

Sauté onion in butter until transparent, stir in flour and slowly add the stock, stirring until boiling. Add tarragon and salt and pepper. Simmer for ½ hour, then cool. Remove fat, pack and freeze.

To serve:

Place soup in a saucepan, and bring slowly to the boil, remove from heat and beat in the egg yolk and cream. Reheat if necessary but do not boil.
Serves 4

Tomato and Mixed Vegetable Soup

1-pound tomatoes (skinned and chopped)
1 onion (chopped)
2 sticks celery (chopped)
2 carrots (scraped and diced)
1 pint beef stock
salt and pepper
1 teaspoon sugar
2 teaspoons tomato purée

Freezer Storage Life: up to 3 months

Preparation for freezing:

Place vegetables in a saucepan and pour stock on top, add salt and pepper and purée. Bring to the boil then cover and simmer until vegetables are cooked. Cool, pack and freeze.

To serve:

Turn soup into a saucepan, bring slowly to the boil, adjust seasoning if necessary.
Serves 4

French Onion Soup

2-pound onions (peeled and chopped)
2-ounce butter
1-ounce flour
salt and pepper
1 teaspoon sugar
1 pint beef stock

To serve:
4 slices French bread
garlic salt
grated cheese
Freezer Storage Life: up to 3 months

Preparation for freezing:

Sauté the onions in butter until beginning to brown (stir frequently to prevent burning). Mix in flour, salt and pepper and sugar, then add stock stirring over heat until boiling; cover and simmer for 20 minutes. Cool, remove any fat from the surface, pack and freeze.

To serve:

Turn soup into a saucepan, and bring to the boil. Toast French bread and sprinkle with a little garlic salt. Serve a piece of toast on top of each soup bowl and sprinkle with grated cheese.
Serves 4

Many of the sauces in this section form the basis of a complete dish. Bolognaise sauce only requires heating through and while this is being done, spaghetti (or other pasta) can be cooked, so providing a quick and tasty meal. Pieces of cold, cooked meat or chicken may be added to the curry sauce, then served with rice. Most sauces freeze well. Two exceptions are mayonnaise and custard-based sauces. They should be packed in $\frac{1}{2}$-pint or 1-pint quantities, with the amount marked on the container, and $\frac{1}{4}-\frac{1}{2}$ inch headspace left at the top. If separation should occur while reheating, careful whisking will restore the correct consistency.

Savoury Sauces

Pancake with Béchamel Sauce (Prawn)
Steak with Pepper Sauce
Courgettes with Béchamel Sauce (Cheese)

Hollandaise Sauce

4 tablespoons wine vinegar
4 egg yolks
4-ounce butter
salt and pepper

Freezer Storage Life for Hollandaise Sauce and all variants: up to 3 months

Preparation for freezing:
Place vinegar in a saucepan, bring to the boil and cook until reduced by half. Measure and add enough cold water to give 3 fluid ounces. Add the egg yolks separately, beating well all the time. Return the sauce to the heat and cook gently until the sauce begins to thicken. Add the butter in small pieces, beating well, until all the butter is blended in. Remove from the heat and add salt and pepper to taste. Cool, pack and freeze.

To serve:
Allow to thaw out for 2–3 hours. If required warm, place the sauce in a basin over a pan of hot water and simmer for a few minutes.

Variations
Béarnaise Sauce
Peel and chop 2 shallots and cook in the vinegar with some fresh herbs (thyme, tarragon, chervil and bay leaf) about 1 tablespoon for 3–4 minutes. Strain the vinegar into a clean saucepan, then continue as above.
Serve with grilled steaks or fish.

Mousseline Sauce
Fold $\frac{1}{4}$ pint whipped cream into Hollandaise sauce just before serving.
Serve with baked fish or vegetables.

Choron Sauce
Add 1 teaspoon tomato purée and 2 teaspoons grated orange rind to the Hollandaise sauce before beating in the butter. Serve with grilled meat or fish.

Neapolitan Sauce

1 onion (chopped)
1 clove garlic (crushed)
1 tablespoon oil
2-pound tomatoes (peeled and quartered)
salt and pepper
1 teaspoon sugar
$\frac{1}{2}$ teaspoon oregano

Freezer Storage Life: up to 3 months

Preparation for freezing:
Fry the onion and garlic in the oil until soft. Add tomatoes and cook for a few minutes. Add rest of the ingredients and simmer for 15 minutes, add a little stock or water if the sauce is too thick and cook for a further 15 minutes. Cool, pack and freeze.

To serve:
Turn the sauce into a saucepan and heat very gently until soft. Raise heat, bring to the boil and cook for a few minutes. Serve with pasta or baked fish.

Cranberry Sauce

1-pound cranberries
$\frac{1}{4}$ pint water
3-4-ounce sugar
$\frac{1}{2}$-ounce butter

Freezer Storage Life: up to 6 months

Preparation for freezing:
Cook the cranberries in the water until soft. Press the fruit juice through a sieve into a clean saucepan. Add the sugar and butter and cook until the sugar has dissolved. Cool, pack and freeze.

To serve:
If serving cold, allow to thaw out overnight in the refrigerator or 2–3 hours at room temperature. If serving hot, turn sauce into a saucepan and heat gently.

Béchamel Sauce

1 small onion (chopped)
1 carrot (chopped)
2 cloves
4 peppercorns
1 bay leaf
1 pint milk
1½-ounce butter
1½-ounce flour
salt and pepper

Freezer Storage Life for Béchamel Sauce and all variants: up to 3 months

Preparation for freezing:
Place the onion, carrot, cloves, peppercorns and bay leaf in a saucepan with the milk, bring almost to the boil and leave in a warm place for 30 minutes to infuse. Strain the milk into a jug. Melt the butter in a saucepan and stir in the flour, add the milk gradually, stirring over heat until the sauce boils. Cook for a few minutes. Add salt and pepper to taste. Cool by placing the saucepan in a little cold water and stir frequently to prevent a skin forming. Pour into ½- or 1-pint containers, leaving ½-inch headspace, cover and freeze.

To serve:
Turn the block into a saucepan (to loosen the sauce, dip container into boiling water for a few minutes), place pan over a low heat and stir occasionally until thawed. Add extra ingredients if required (see below) and cook for 2–3 minutes, stirring.

Variations
Cheese sauce:
Add 4-ounce grated cheese and 1 teaspoon made mustard.

Parsley sauce:
Add 2 tablespoons chopped parsley.

Mushroom sauce:
Wipe and slice 4-ounce mushrooms. Fry in a little butter and add to the sauce.

Prawn sauce:
Add 2-ounce peeled prawns and a dash of anchovy essence.

Apple Sauce

1-pound cooking apples (peeled, cored and sliced)
water
2-3-ounce sugar
3-4 cloves (optional)
1-ounce butter

Freezer Storage Life: up to 6 months

Preparation for freezing:
Cook the apples and cloves, if used, in a little water until soft. Drain off the water, remove cloves, add sugar and butter and cook until sugar is dissolved.
Serve as for Cranberry Sauce on page 56.

Sauce Bordelaise

1 onion (chopped)
1 clove garlic (crushed)
1 tablespoon oil
¼ pint beef stock
¼ pint red wine

Beurre manié:
1-ounce butter
1-ounce flour
salt and pepper

To serve:
¼ pint red wine
Freezer Storage Life: up to 2 months

Preparation for freezing:
Fry the onion and garlic in the oil for a few minutes. Add the stock and red wine, bring to the boil and cook for 20 minutes. Mix the butter and flour together and add it, a little at a time, to the sauce, cook for a further 2–3 minutes. Add salt and pepper to taste. Cool, remove any excess fat, pack and freeze.

To serve:
Turn out into a saucepan and heat gently until soft. Add the extra ¼ pint wine and boil quickly for 3 minutes.
Serve with steaks or roast beef.

Sweet and Sour Sauce

1 onion (chopped)
1 tablespoon oil
1 stick celery (chopped)
1 carrot (scraped and sliced)
1 tablespoon demerara sugar
1 teaspoon mustard
3 teaspoons tomato purée
½ pint pineapple juice
2 tablespoons vinegar
1 tablespoon lemon juice
salt and pepper

Freezer Storage Life: up to 3 months

Preparation for freezing:
Fry the onion in the oil for a few minutes, add the celery and carrot and fry for 2–3 minutes. Stir in the rest of the ingredients, and simmer for 30 minutes.
If preferred the sauce may be sieved or blended. Cool, pack and freeze.

To serve:
Turn the sauce into a saucepan and cook over low heat until soft, then bring to the boil.
Serve with pork spareribs or chops.

Bread Sauce

1 pint milk
1 onion (chopped)
3-4 cloves
4-ounce white breadcrumbs
1-ounce butter
salt and pepper

Freezer Storage Life: up to 2 months

Preparation for freezing:
Place milk, onion and cloves in a saucepan. Bring to the boil then leave in a warm place for at least ½ hour to infuse. Strain milk into another saucepan stir in the breadcrumbs and butter and cook over gentle heat for 10 minutes. Add salt and pepper to taste. Cool, pack and freeze.

To serve:
Turn sauce into a saucepan or casserole and cook gently on top of cooker or in the oven until hot. Stir occasionally to prevent sticking.
Serve with roast chicken or turkey.

Above, also shows Cranberry Sauce, recipe see page 56

Curry Sauce

1 onion (chopped)
1 clove garlic (crushed)
1-ounce butter
1-2 tablespoons curry powder
1 cooking apple (peeled, cored and sliced)
½ pint stock
2 teaspoons chutney
salt and pepper

Freezer Storage Life: up to 2 months

Preparation for freezing:
Fry the onion and garlic in the butter until transparent. Stir in the curry powder (use more for a hotter flavour) and fry for 2 minutes. Add the remaining ingredients and simmer for 20 minutes. Sieve or blend the sauce, cool, pack and freeze.

To serve:
Turn out into a saucepan and cook over low heat until soft, boil for 2–3 minutes. Serve with cooked meat or chicken.
Or, allow sauce to soften, add to the pre-fried chicken, beef etc., place in a casserole and cook in the oven until the meat is tender.

Bolognaise Sauce

1 onion (chopped)
1 tablespoon oil
½-pound minced beef
2 teaspoons flour
¼-pound mushrooms (finely chopped)
14-ounce tin tomatoes
1 tablespoon tomato purée
1 teaspoon sugar
¼ pint beef stock
salt and pepper
1 tablespoon sherry

Freezer Storage Life: up to 3 months

Preparation for freezing:
Fry the onion in the oil until soft. Add the mince, break up with a fork, and fry until brown. Stir in the flour and add the rest of the ingredients. Bring to the boil, cover and simmer for 30 minutes. Cool, pack in containers, cover and freeze.

To serve:
Reheat in a saucepan on top of the cooker or in a casserole in the oven.
Serve with boiled spaghetti.

Orange Sauce

1 onion (chopped)
1 tablespoon oil
grated rind of 2 and juice of 3 oranges
¼ pint stock
2 teaspoons cornflour
salt and pepper
1 tablespoon redcurrant jelly

Freezer Storage Life: up to 3 months

Preparation for freezing:
Fry the onion in the oil until soft. Add orange rind, juice and stock, bring to the boil. Blend the cornflour in a little cold water and stir into the hot liquid, cook for a few minutes until thick. Add salt and pepper to taste, cover the pan and simmer for 15 minutes. Stir in the redcurrant jelly and leave to cool. Pack in containers, cover and freeze.

To serve:
Reheat in a saucepan—or if using for a duck or chicken casserole, leave until softened and pour over the pre-fried duck or chicken pieces and cook in a casserole for 1½ hours, or until the meat is cooked.

Pepper Sauce

1 onion (chopped)
1 green pepper (deseeded and chopped)
3½-ounce tin pimentos (chopped)
1-ounce butter
1 tablespoon flour
1 pint chicken stock
½ teaspoon paprika
salt

Freezer Storage Life: up to 3 months

Preparation for freezing:
Place onion, green peppers and pimentos in a saucepan, add the butter and cook until vegetables begin to soften. Stir in the flour and gradually add the stock. Bring to the boil, add paprika and salt to taste, then simmer for 30 minutes.
If preferred the sauce may be sieved or blended. Cool, pack and freeze.

To serve:
Turn the sauce into a saucepan and cook over low heat until soft, boil for 2–3 minutes.
Serve with grilled steaks or lamb chops.

Cumberland Sauce

2 oranges
½ pint water
juice 1 lemon
1 tablespoon Worcestershire sauce
2 teaspoons cornflour
½ pound redcurrant jelly
4 tablespoons port
salt and pepper
6-8 glacé cherries (chopped)

Freezer Storage Life: up to 3 months

Preparation for freezing:
Remove thin strips of rind from the oranges, then boil rind in the water until soft. Add the lemon juice, Worcestershire sauce and bring to the boil. Blend the cornflour in a little cold water, stir into the orange liquid and cook until thickened. Add the remaining ingredients and cook, stirring, until the redcurrant jelly has dissolved.
Allow to cool, then pack and freeze.

To serve:
Allow to thaw out for 2–3 hours at room temperature, or overnight in refrigerator.
Serve with cold meats or pâté.

Only really fresh fish and shell fish should be frozen at home. The freshness of the fish can usually be recognised by the firmness of the flesh, bright eyes and scales. Fish which has a strong, stale smell should not be used in dishes for freezing. A reliable fishmonger will advise on the 'best buy' in variety and price. Prepare the dishes as soon as possible after purchase. Fish dishes, frozen in a sauce, freeze and have a longer storage life than plain cooked whole fish or fillets. In the following recipes, commercially frozen fish fillets and steaks can be used, providing they have only just thawed. The dish should be prepared and cooked immediately, then frozen.

Fish

Smoked Fish Kedgeree
Coquilles St Jacques
Prawn Croquettes

62

Russian Fish Pie

1-pound white fish (cod, haddock etc.)
2 hard-boiled eggs
¾ pint Béchamel sauce (see page 57)
1 teaspoon grated lemon rind
pinch cayenne pepper
2 teaspoons chopped parsley
13-ounce packet frozen puff pastry (thawed)

To serve:
milk *or* beaten egg
Freezer Storage Life: up to 3 months

Preparation for freezing:
Poach the fish in a little water. Drain well and remove any skin and bones. Flake the fish into a basin. Chop the hard-boiled eggs and mix with the fish. Add sauce, lemon rind, cayenne pepper and parsley. Roll the pastry to a square 10 by 10 inches. Place the fish mixture in the centre and brush edges of the pastry with milk or beaten egg. Fold the corners of the pastry into the centre (like an envelope). Place the pie in the freezer until hard, then wrap and freeze.

To serve:
Remove wrapping and place the pie on a baking tray. Brush with milk or beaten egg and bake at 425°F/Gas 7 for 45–60 minutes.
Serves 6

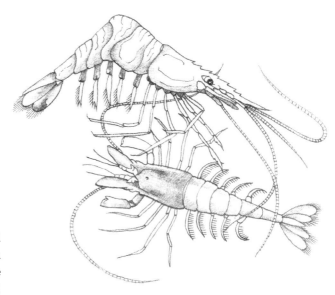

Prawn Croquettes

2-ounce butter
2-ounce flour
½ pint milk
8-ounce peeled prawns
salt and pepper
1 teaspoon onion (grated)
1 teaspoon lemon juice
1 egg yolk
1 egg
browned breadcrumbs

Freezer Storage Life: up to 3 months

Preparation for freezing:
Make a thick white sauce with the butter, flour and milk. Roughly chop the prawns and mix into the sauce with salt, pepper, lemon juice and grated onion. Mix in the egg yolk and leave until cold. Divide the mixture into pieces and form into cork shapes. Lightly beat the egg and dip the croquettes into it, then coat in breadcrumbs.
Pack in flat containers with a piece of foil between layers. Cover, seal and freeze.

To serve:
Fry in deep fat or oil. If cooking while still frozen, make sure the fat or oil isn't too hot, otherwise the outside will brown before the inside is cooked. Drain on kitchen paper before serving.
Serves 4

Smoked Fish Kedgeree

8-ounce long-grain rice
12-ounce smoked haddock
2-ounce butter
salt and pepper
1 teaspoon grated lemon rind

To serve:
2 hard-boiled eggs
parsley (chopped)
Freezer Storage Life: up to 3 months

Preparation for freezing:
Cook rice in boiling salted water for 8 minutes until just cooked, then drain well. Poach the fish in a little water, drain and flake. Melt the butter and mix into the rice with salt, pepper and lemon rind. Gently stir in fish. Place in containers, cover, seal and freeze.

To serve:
Allow kedgeree to thaw out slightly, then turn into an oven-proof dish. Garnish with hard-boiled eggs and a little chopped parsley. Cover and heat through in the oven, 350°F/Gas 4 for 30–40 minutes.
Serves 4

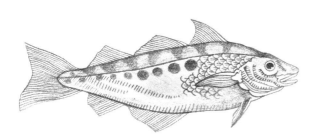

Stuffed Halibut Steaks

4 halibut steaks
1 small onion (finely chopped)
2 teaspoons oil
2-ounce white breadcrumbs
pinch ground bay leaf
salt and pepper
1 egg yolk

Freezer Storage Life: up to 3 months

Preparation for freezing:
Remove centre bones from halibut. Fry onion in oil until soft, add crumbs, bay leaf, salt and pepper and bind with egg yolk. Fill the cavity left by the bone with the stuffing and spread over the steaks. Wrap in freezer foil and freeze.

To serve:
Place steaks in a shallow oven-proof dish, brush each one with oil and pour a little white wine (or milk) into the dish. Cover and bake at 325°F/Gas 3 for 40 minutes.
Serves 4

Sweet Corn Fish Cakes

1-pound cod
1-pound potatoes (cooked and mashed)
10½-ounce tin creamed sweet corn
1 tablespoon chopped parsley
salt and pepper
2 teaspoons Tabasco sauce
browned breadcrumbs

Freezer Storage Life: up to 3 months

Preparation for freezing:
Poach the cod in salted water, drain, remove any skin and bones and flake into a basin. Mix in the potato and creamed sweet corn. Add chopped parsley, salt, pepper and Tabasco sauce. Chill until firm. Divide the mixture into pieces and form into cakes. Coat in browned crumbs. Place in a shallow container with a piece of foil between each layer. Cover, seal and freeze.

To serve:
Fry in shallow fat for about 10 minutes, turning once, until crisp and golden.
Serves 6

Fish Pudding au Gratin

1-pound cod
2 eggs
$\frac{1}{4}$ pint milk
2-ounce white breadcrumbs
pinch cayenne pepper
salt and pepper
1 tablespoon melted butter

To serve:
$\frac{1}{4}$ pint cheese sauce (see page 57)
brown breadcrumbs
grated cheese
pieces of toast
parsley
Freezer Storage Life: up to 3 months

Preparation for freezing:
Poach the fish in a little water, then drain well. Remove any skin and bones and flake fish finely. Separate the eggs and mix yolks with the milk, add breadcrumbs and leave to soak for 10 minutes. Combine fish, crumb mixture, cayenne pepper, salt, pepper and melted butter. Whisk egg whites until stiff and fold into the fish. Spoon into a buttered 2-pint soufflé dish or pudding basin. Cover with freezer foil, seal, freeze.

To serve:
Remove from freezer and leave to stand for 30 minutes. Remove foil and bake at 350°F/Gas 4 for 1–1$\frac{1}{4}$ hours, or until cooked through to the centre. Pour the cheese sauce over the top and sprinkle with breadcrumbs and grated cheese. Brown under the grill. Arrange the pieces of toast round edge of dish and garnish with parsley.
Serves 4

Crab Cocottes

2 (3-ounce) tins crab meat
1-ounce butter
1-ounce flour
$\frac{1}{4}$ pint fish stock (liquid from tinned crab and water)
$\frac{1}{4}$ pint cream *or* milk
1 tablespoon dry vermouth (optional)
4-ounce mushrooms (sliced)
salt and pepper
2-ounce white breadcrumbs
little butter

Freezer Storage Life: up to 3 months

Preparation for freezing:
Drain liquid from the crab, remove any slivers of bone, and flake the fish. Melt the butter in a saucepan and stir in the flour. Add the stock gradually, bring to the boil stirring until thick, add the cream or milk, vermouth (if used) and mushrooms and cook for 3 minutes. Stir crab into the sauce with salt and pepper to taste. Butter 4 individual cocotte dishes or foil containers and spoon the crab mixture into these. Cool. Sprinkle with the breadcrumbs and dot with a little butter. Cover with foil, seal and freeze.

To serve:
Place dishes on a baking tray, bake at 350°F/Gas 4, for 20 minutes, remove the foil covering and bake for 10 minutes, until golden brown.
Serves 4

Sole Bonne Femme

8 fillets sole
¼ pint white wine
¼ pint water
½-pound mushrooms (sliced)
salt and pepper
Beurre manié (see method)

To serve:
1 tablespoon lemon juice
2 tablespoons double cream
Freezer Storage Life: up to 3 months

Preparation for freezing:
Place the fish in a shallow pan and pour the wine
and water on top. Add the mushrooms and salt
and pepper to taste. Simmer the fish for about
10 minutes, or until cooked. Drain fish and place
in freezer container. Make *beurre manié* by
blending ½-ounce butter with ¾-ounce flour then
add gradually to the liquid in the pan. Boil and
stir until thickened, cool and pour over the fish.
Pack and freeze.

To serve:
Reheat the fish in a covered dish in the oven. When
the sauce is hot stir in the lemon juice and cream.
Serves 4

Prawns with Tomato Cream Sauce

1 small onion (chopped)
1 tablespoon oil
8-ounce tin tomatoes
1 tablespoon tomato purée
¼ teaspoon basil
pinch sugar
salt and pepper
12-ounce peeled prawns (or scampi)

To serve:
4 tablespoons cream
cooked long-grain rice
Freezer Storage Life: up to 3 months

Preparation for freezing:
Fry the onion in the oil until transparent. Add the
tomatoes and mash with a fork. Stir in the other
ingredients except for the prawns and cream, and
simmer for 15 minutes. Add the prawns and cook
for a further 5 minutes. Cool, pack and freeze.

To serve:
Reheat in a saucepan or in the oven and when
bubbling stir in the cream. Serve with plain
boiled rice.
Serves 4

Above, also shows Russian Fish Pie, recipe
see page 64

Haddock Duglère

1 onion (finely chopped)
1 tablespoon oil
14-ounce tin tomatoes
4-ounce mushrooms (sliced)
salt and pepper
1½-pound haddock fillets
¼ pint water
¼ pint dry white wine
1 tablespoon chopped parsley
pinch tarragon

Freezer Storage Life: up to 3 months

Preparation for freezing:
Sauté onion in the oil until softened, add tomatoes, mushrooms, salt and pepper and cook gently for 15 minutes. Meanwhile poach fish in the water and wine until just cooked (about 7 minutes). Drain the fish, remove the skin and leave to cool. Reduce fish cooking-liquid to half by boiling quickly, strain into the tomato sauce and add parsley and tarragon. Bring to the boil, remove from the heat and cool quickly. Place fish in container, cover with sauce, pack, seal and freeze.

To serve:
Remove foil from the frozen block. Place the block in an oven-proof casserole. Cover and bake at 350°F/Gas 4 until bubbling hot (about 1 hour).
Serves 4

Prawn Risotto

1 onion (chopped)
½-ounce butter
1 tablespoon oil
4-ounce mushrooms (sliced)
¼ pint chicken stock
2-ounce long-grain rice
salt and pepper
pinch powdered bay leaf
8-ounce peeled prawns

To serve:
parsley (chopped)
lemon slices
Freezer Storage Life: up to 3 months

Preparation for freezing:
Fry the onion in the butter and oil until soft. Add the mushrooms and other ingredients except the prawns. Cook over low heat for about 20–25 minutes until the liquid is absorbed and rice is cooked. Stir in the prawns. Pack, seal and freeze.

To serve:
Allow the risotto to soften for about an hour (or overnight in the refrigerator). Melt 1-ounce butter in a saucepan and add the risotto. Cook over very low heat, stirring occasionally, until hot. Serve on a heated serving dish garnished with chopped parsley and lemon slices.
Serves 4

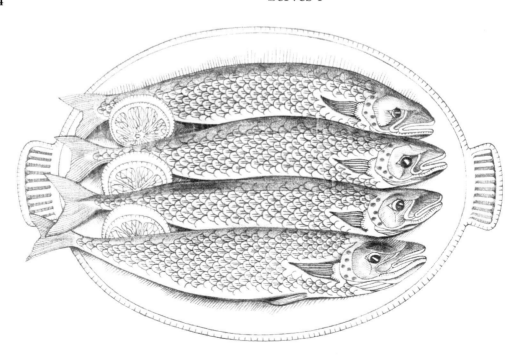

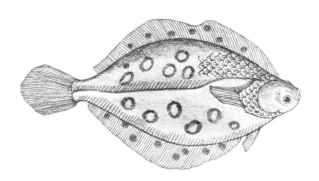

Halibut with Lemon Sauce

¼ pint lemon juice (approx. 4 lemons)
¼ pint water
2 teaspoons chopped parsley
4 halibut steaks *N.B. cod is equally good*
salt and pepper

Sauce:
1½-ounce butter
1½-ounce flour
¼ pint milk
¼ pint cream

Freezer Storage Life: up to 3 months

Preparation for freezing:
Put lemon juice, water and parsley into a large frying-pan. Place the fish in the liquid and sprinkle with salt and pepper. Cover the pan and poach the fish for 10–15 minutes (the fish is cooked when the skin is easily removable). Drain fish and strain the liquid into a jug. Remove skin and centre bone from the fish and place fish in freezer container. For the sauce, melt the butter in a saucepan and stir in the flour. Add the reserved fish liquid and the milk slowly, stirring over heat until thick. Boil for 2–3 minutes and stir in the cream. Cool, then spoon over the fish. Cover, seal and freeze.

To serve:
Place the covered container in the oven, at 325°F/Gas 3, and cook for 30 minutes. Remove cover and continue cooking until hot throughout.
Serves 4

Plaice Thermidor

8 fillets plaice
1 small onion (chopped)
1-ounce butter
1 tablespoon cornflour
¼ pint milk
¼ pint white wine
1 tablespoon brandy (optional)
½ teaspoon made mustard
salt and pepper
3 tablespoons double cream
1-ounce grated Parmesan cheese

To serve:
extra Parmesan cheese
Freezer Storage Life: up to 3 months

Preparation for freezing:
Remove skin from the plaice, poach in a little water for 5 minutes. Drain and place in oven-proof or foil dish. Fry the onion in butter until transparent, stir in the cornflour, add milk and cook until thickened, stir in wine and brandy (if used) and boil for 2 minutes. Add mustard, salt, pepper, cream and cheese. Pour sauce over the fish. Cover with freezer foil and seal.

To serve:
If still frozen, leave foil on and reheat in the oven at 350°F/Gas 4 for 30 minutes. Remove foil, sprinkle with extra Parmesan cheese and cook for a further 15 minutes or until hot.
Serves 4

Scallops Gratinées

8 scallops
¼ pint water
¼ pint white wine
1 small onion (chopped)
½-pound mushrooms (chopped)
2 tablespoons oil
1 tablespoon parsley (chopped)
salt and pepper
white breadcrumbs

Freezer Storage Life: up to 3 months

Preparation for freezing:
If the scallops are in shells, remove them, wash and
keep the shells. Rinse scallops in cold water and
place in a saucepan. Add water and wine, bring to
the boil and cook for 10 minutes. Meanwhile fry
onion and mushrooms in oil until soft. Drain off
excess oil and mix parsley, salt and pepper with
the mushrooms and onion. Place a spoonful of this
mixture into each of the 4 shells, individual oven-
proof or foil dishes. Place two drained scallops
in each dish and cover with remaining mushroom
mixture. Sprinkle with breadcrumbs. Cover each
dish with freezer foil and seal.

To serve:
If these are reheated straight from the freezer,
leave foil on and place in the oven, 350°F/Gas 4 for
30 minutes. Remove foil, sprinkle with more breadcrumbs and dot with butter. Place under a hot
grill to crisp the crumbs.
Serves 4

Coquilles St Jacques

Preparation for freezing:
Prepare and cook scallops as above. Drain and
place in shells or oven-proof dishes. Make a sauce
with the reserved cooking liquid: blend 1 tablespoon cornflour with a little milk. Stir into hot
liquid and cook until thick. Add ½-ounce butter,
1-ounce grated cheese, two tablespoons cream and
one egg yolk. Pour sauce over the scallops and
sprinkle with grated cheese. Cover with freezer
foil.

To serve:
Heat and serve as above. If liked, a border of
mashed cooked potato can be piped around the
scallops before browning under the grill.
Serves 4

Tomato Fish Pie

6-ounce long-grain rice
1½ pint chicken stock *or* water and stock cubes
2¼-ounce tin tomato purée
1 teaspoon sugar
½ teaspoon dried basil
¼ teaspoon pepper
1½-pound white fish (cod, haddock, etc.)
2 tomatoes (skinned and sliced)

To serve:
grated cheese
Freezer Storage Life: up to 3 months

Preparation for freezing:
Cook the rice in the chicken stock for about 8 minutes. Put the tomato purée into another saucepan, with sugar, basil and pepper. Cut fish into pieces and cook gently in the tomato mixture. Drain the rice and place in oven-proof dish or foil container. Pour the fish and tomato mixture over the rice, cover with slices of tomato. Cover with freezer foil and seal.

To serve:
If still frozen, leave foil on and reheat in the oven, 375°F/Gas 5 for 45 minutes. Remove foil and sprinkle top of pie with grated cheese. Return to the oven for a further 20 minutes until cheese is golden brown.
Serves 4–6

Sole Béarnaise

8 fillets sole
1 small onion (chopped)
1 stick celery (chopped)
1 bay leaf
salt and pepper
¾ pint milk
1 tablespoon cornflour
1-ounce butter
1 tablespoon vinegar
2 tablespoons dry white wine
1 shallot (chopped)
2 egg yolks
½-ounce butter

Freezer Storage Life: up to 3 months

Preparation for freezing:
Fold the fillets in half and arrange in an oven-proof dish. Pour a little water into the dish, cover and cook fish at 350°F/Gas 4 for 20 minutes. Meanwhile put onion, celery, bay leaf, little salt and pepper into a saucepan with the milk. Bring almost to the boil, then leave in a warm place for ½ hour to infuse. Strain milk into another pan, add the cornflour blended with 2 tablespoons milk or water and cook until thick. Add the butter. In a separate saucepan, boil vinegar, wine and shallot. When reduced to half quantity, strain and return to the pan. Beat in the sauce, egg yolks and butter. Drain liquid from the fish and pour sauce over the top. Cover with freezer foil and seal.

To serve:
If thawed, remove foil and reheat in the oven for 15 minutes. If still hard, leave foil on and cook for 30 minutes at 325°F/Gas 3. Remove foil, raise oven temperature to 375°F/Gas 5 and cook until hot. (*Note:* if sauce separates, stir gently to blend.)
Serves 4

It is better to freeze large joints and poultry uncooked, providing sufficient time has been allowed for thawing. This is particularly important when cooking poultry. Small, thinner pieces of meat can be cooked while still hard, so it is advisable to pack them interleaved with foil or polythene for ease of separation. Cooked meat and poultry dishes freeze well and are convenient to have in the freezer as they only need reheating before serving. The preparation of casseroles, pies and meat loaves are time-consuming, but making extra quantities takes little extra time—well worth while for working wives and those who entertain at home.

Meat

Chicken with Oranges
Carbonnade of Beef
Spareribs with Pineapple Sweet and
Sour Sauce

Boeuf Stroganoff

1½-pound rump steak
1-ounce butter
1 tablespoon oil
2 onions (chopped)
1 clove garlic (crushed)
2 tablespoons flour
2 tablespoons tomato purée
4 tablespoons tomato ketchup
2-3 tablespoons paprika
salt and pepper
¼ pint red wine
¼-½ pint stock

To serve:
½ pint double cream
Freezer Storage Life: up to 3 months

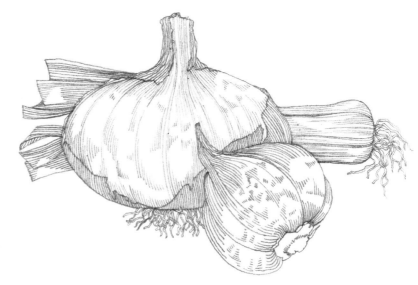

Preparation for freezing:
Cut the steak into thin strips and fry in butter and oil until brown. Drain and place meat in a saucepan. Fry onions and garlic in remaining fat, drain and add to the meat. Stir in the flour and cook for a minute until blended. Add the remaining ingredients, bring to the boil and cook quickly for a few minutes. Reduce heat, cover the pan and leave to simmer for about ¾ hour. Cool and remove any fat from the top. Pack and freeze.

To serve:
Place stroganoff into a saucepan and bring slowly to the boil, stir in the cream and when hot (but not boiling) serve.
Serves 4–6

Carbonnade of Beef

2-pound chuck steak
1-ounce flour
salt and pepper
2 tablespoons oil
4 carrots (sliced)
2 onions (chopped)
¼-pound mushrooms (sliced)
2¼-ounce tin tomato purée
½ pint brown ale
¼ pint stock

To serve:
parsley (chopped)
Freezer Storage Life: up to 3 months

Preparation for freezing:
Cut meat into cubes and coat in flour mixed with a little salt and pepper. Fry meat in the oil until brown then transfer to an oven-proof casserole. Mix in the carrots, onions and mushrooms. Add the tomato purée, brown ale and stock. Bring to the boil and pour into the casserole. Cover and cook at 325°F/Gas 3 for 2–2½ hours. Cool, remove excess fat, pack and freeze.

To serve:
Reheat in a casserole in the oven or saucepan on top of the cooker. Sprinkle with chopped parsley.
Serves 6

Chicken Curry

(This recipe can also be made with beef or lamb)

4 chicken pieces *or* **1-pound lean beef** *or* **lamb**
1 tablespoon oil
½-ounce butter
1 onion (chopped)
1 clove garlic (crushed)
1-2 tablespoons curry powder
8-ounce tin tomatoes
salt and pepper
¼ teaspoon chilli powder (optional)

Freezer Storage Life: up to 2 months

Preparation for freezing:
Remove skin from the chicken, or cut beef or lamb into pieces. Fry the chicken or meat in oil until brown then transfer to an oven-proof casserole. Fry the onion, garlic and curry powder in the butter and remaining oil for 5 minutes, drain off excess oil. Add the tomatoes, chilli powder and seasoning, cook for a minute or two then pour over the chicken. Cover and cook at 350°F/Gas 4 for 50–60 minutes until chicken or meat is tender. Check while the dish is cooking and if dry add a little stock. Cool, pack and freeze.

To serve:
Reheat in the oven or on top of the cooker for about 40 minutes.
Serves 4

Chicken with Oranges

4 chicken quarters
1-ounce butter
1 onion (chopped)
3½-ounce tin pimentos
grated rind and juice 2 oranges
¼ pint chicken stock
pinch chilli powder
salt and pepper

To serve:
plain boiled rice
2 teaspoons redcurrant jelly
Freezer Storage Life: up to 3 months

Preparation for freezing:
Remove skin from the chicken quarters, then sauté chicken in butter until lightly browned. Place in an oven-proof casserole. Sauté onion and add to chicken. Drain pimentos, chop and add to the casserole. Mix orange rind, juice and stock with chilli powder and salt and pepper. Pour on to the chicken, cover and cook at 350°F/Gas 4 for 1 hour. Cool, pack and freeze.

To serve:
Remove chicken from container and place in a casserole. Cook at 325°F/Gas 3 until thawed, raise oven temperature to 375°F/Gas 5. Add redcurrant jelly to chicken and cook for a further 15–20 minutes until hot. Serve with plain boiled rice.
Serves 4

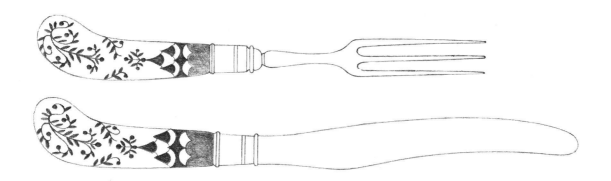

Beef Olives

8 thin slices topside or rump steak
seasoned flour
1 ounce fat or oil
$\frac{3}{4}$ pint beef stock
2 onions (sliced)
pepper and salt

Stuffing:
5 ounce fresh breadcrumbs
4 ounce mushrooms (finely chopped)
grated rind $\frac{1}{2}$ lemon
pepper and salt
beaten egg to mix
$\frac{1}{2}$ ounce butter

Freezer Storage Life: up to 3 months

Preparation for freezing:
Melt butter in frying pan and lightly fry mushrooms. Add to the breadcrumbs and combine with rest of ingredients for stuffing. Spread each slice of meat with stuffing, roll up, secure with fine string or thread, and toss in seasoned flour.
Heat the fat or oil in the frying pan and brown beef olives lightly, remove and place in casserole.
Add 1 tablespoon of the seasoned flour to the frying pan, brown well, gradually add the stock and bring to the boil. Season to taste and pour over the olives. Add the onion in slices, cover and cook at 350°F/Gas 4 for $1\frac{1}{2}$ hours.
Cool, pack and freeze.

To serve:
Reheat in a saucepan for about 30 minutes until the meat is hot throughout.
Serves 4

Pork with Tomato and Pepper Sauce

Pork with Tomato and Pepper Sauce

4 loin pork chops
1 onion (chopped)
1-pound tomatoes (skinned and chopped)
1 green pepper (deseeded and chopped)
1 teaspoon Tabasco sauce
¼ pint stock
pinch basil
½ teaspoon sugar
salt and pepper

Freezer Storage Life: up to 3 months

Preparation for freezing:
Grill or fry the chops until cooked, drain and when cool place in a container (wax or foil). Fry the onion in the fat left over after cooking the chops, add tomatoes, green pepper, Tabasco, stock, basil, sugar, salt and pepper. Bring to the boil then simmer for 10 minutes. Cool quickly and pour over the chops. Cover and freeze.

To serve:
Turn into a saucepan and bring slowly to the boil. Simmer for 10 minutes to make sure chops are hot throughout.
Serves 4

Chinese Chicken

8 joints chicken
2 tablespoons oil
1 clove garlic (crushed)
6 shallots (peeled)
2 tablespoons soy sauce
2 tablespoons orange juice
2 teaspoons cornflour
¼ pint chicken stock
12-ounce tin bean shoots
salt and pepper

To serve:
plain boiled *or* fried rice
Freezer Storage Life: up to 3 months

Preparation for freezing:
Fry the chicken joints in the oil until golden brown, add the garlic and shallots and fry for another 2–3 minutes. Stir in the soy sauce and orange juice. Blend the cornflour with the stock and stir into the sauce, bring to the boil, stirring until thickened, cover and simmer for ¾ hour (check occasionally—if too dry add extra stock). Drain the bean-shoots and add these to the pan. Cool, then pack and freeze.

To serve:
Reheat in a saucepan over a low heat, or in a casserole in the oven. Serve with plain boiled or fried rice.
Serves 4

Lamb and Mint Pie

1½-pound lean lamb
1-ounce flour
salt and pepper
½-pound carrots
1 tablespoon oil
1 onion (chopped)
4 tablespoons chopped mint
½ pint stock
7½-ounce packet frozen puff pastry

To serve:
beaten egg *or* milk
Freezer Storage Life: up to 3 months

Preparation for freezing:
Cut the lamb into pieces, then coat in flour with salt and pepper. Scrape and slice carrots. Heat oil in a saucepan and fry the onion for a few minutes, add the lamb and fry until brown. Add the carrots, mint and stock, cover the pan and simmer for 40 minutes. Leave to cool and place in a 2-pint pie-dish. Roll out the pastry and use to cover the pie. Wrap and freeze.

To serve:
Glaze top of pastry with beaten egg or milk. Bake at 350°F/Gas 4 for 20 minutes, raise temperature to 400°F/Gas 6 and bake for a further 20 minutes. (If pastry starts to brown too quickly, cover with a piece of foil.)
Serves 4–6

Stuffed Liver

1-pound calves' liver
little flour
1 onion (finely chopped)
2 rashers bacon (chopped)
2-ounce white breadcrumbs
1 teaspoon sage
2 teaspoons chopped parsley
salt and pepper
½ pint stock

Freezer Storage Life: up to 3 months

Preparation for freezing:
Cut liver into pieces and coat in flour. Place half the liver in an oven-proof casserole. Mix the onion, bacon, breadcrumbs, sage, parsley and salt and pepper together. Moisten with a little of the stock then spread this over the liver, top with remaining liver and add remaining stock. Cover and cook at 350°F/Gas 4 for ¾ hour. Cool, pack and freeze.

To serve:
Reheat in a casserole in the oven at 375°F/Gas 5 for 1–1½ hours until hot throughout.
Serves 4

Steak, Kidney and Mushroom Pie

1-pound chuck steak
3 lamb kidneys
1 tablespoon oil
2 onions (chopped)
¾ pint beef stock
salt and pepper
1-2 tablespoons cornflour
¼-pound mushrooms (sliced)
8-ounce shortcrust pastry

Freezer Storage Life: up to 3 months

Preparation for freezing:
Cut steak into cubes. Halve kidneys and remove skins and membranes. Heat the oil in a saucepan and fry the steak for 5 minutes. Add kidneys and onion and fry for 2 minutes, add the stock and seasoning. Cover the pan and simmer for 45–60 minutes until meat is tender. Add the mushrooms. Blend cornflour with a little cold water and stir into the meat. Bring to the boil and cook for 3 minutes. Leave to cool and place in a 2-pint pie-dish. Roll out the pastry and cover the pie. Pack and freeze.

To serve:
Bake at 350°F/Gas 4 for 20 minutes, then raise temperature to 400°F/Gas 6 and bake for a further 20 minutes.
Serves 4

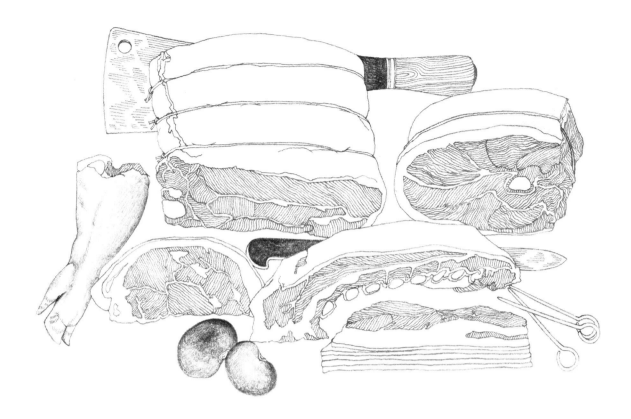

Irish Stew

2-pound neck of lamb
3 onions (chopped)
2-pound potatoes (peeled and sliced)
salt and pepper
½ pint water or stock

To serve:
parsley (chopped)
Freezer Storage Life: up to 3 months

Preparation for freezing:
Trim any surplus fat from the meat and cut meat
into pieces. Arrange the meat, onions and potatoes in layers in an oven-proof casserole. Add the
seasoning and stock. Cover and cook at 325°F/
Gas 3 for 3 hours. Cool, remove excess fat from
the top. Pack and freeze.

To serve:
Place in a casserole and reheat at 325°F/Gas 3
until hot all through. Serve sprinkled with
chopped parsley.
Serves 6

Shepherd's Pie

1½-pound minced steak
1 onion (chopped)
1-ounce fat
½-pound tomatoes (skinned and sliced)
1-ounce porridge oats
salt and pepper
1 beef stock cube
¼ pint water
1-pound cooked potato (mashed)

Freezer Storage Life: up to 3 months

Preparation for freezing:
Fry the mince and onion in the fat until brown.
Drain off the fat and add tomatoes, porridge oats,
salt, pepper, stock cube and water. Cook over
gentle heat for ¾ hour. Leave to cool and place in a
pie-dish. Pipe or spread the potato on top of the
meat. Pack and freeze.
To serve:
Reheat in the oven 325°F/Gas 3 for 40 minutes.
Raise temperature to 400°F/Gas 6 and cook for a
further 25–30 minutes until golden brown.
Serves 6

Baked Meat Loaf

2 teaspoons dried pepper flakes
1-pound minced beef
1 onion (chopped)
2-ounce white breadcrumbs
salt and pepper
1-ounce margarine
1 egg

Freezer Storage Life: up to 3 months

Preparation for freezing:
Soak pepper flakes in water for 20 minutes. Mix mince, onion and breadcrumbs together. Drain pepper flakes and add to the mince mixture. Add salt, pepper, margarine and beaten egg. Spoon this into a greased 1-pound loaf-tin and cover with foil. Place tin in a roasting-tin with a little water in the base. Cook at 350°F/Gas 4 for 1½ hours. Cool in tin, then turn out, pack and freeze.

To serve:
Cold:—leave to thaw completely for 4 hours or overnight in the refrigerator. Garnish with hard-boiled egg.
Hot:—leave to soften slightly (about 1 hour) place in the loaf tin, cover and reheat in the oven.
Serves 6
Above, also shows Pork and Sausage Casserole, recipe see page 84

Chicken Kiev

4 breasts of chicken
3 tablespoons chopped chives *or* parsley
4-ounce butter
salt and pepper
2 tablespoons lemon juice
2 eggs (beaten)
6-ounce white breadcrumbs

Freezer Storage Life: up to 6 months

Preparation for freezing:
Using a sharp pointed knife, carefully remove the chicken flesh from the bones, taking care not to pierce the flesh. Press the pieces of chicken out flat. Cream the butter with the chives or parsley, salt, pepper and lemon juice, form into four pieces and chill. Place a piece of the butter in the centre of each piece of chicken, fold the narrow ends of the chicken into the centre and fold over. Dip each piece of chicken in the beaten egg and coat in crumbs, pat these well on and repeat the process to double coat. Pack and freeze.

To serve:
Allow to thaw for about 1 hour, fry first in a cool deep fat, remove, heat fat and fry quickly until golden brown.
Serves 4

American-Style Hamburgers

1-pound minced beef
1 onion (finely chopped)
½ clove garlic (crushed)
salt and pepper
1 tablespoon tomato purée

To serve:
little fat *or* oil
Freezer Storage Life: up to 2 months

Preparation for freezing:
Mix the minced beef with the other ingredients
and blend well together. Divide the mixture into
eight pieces and form into patties. Pack and freeze.

To serve:
Heat a little fat or oil in a frying-pan. If the ham-
burgers are cooked straight from the freezer, fry
gently to allow the insides to cook. Test with a
skewer and if still hard fry for a few minutes
longer. Depending on thickness they will take
7–10 minutes each side.
Serves 4

Cornish Pasty

Short-crust pastry:
4-ounce plain flour
1-ounce margarine
1-ounce lard
pinch salt
water to mix to a firm dough
Filling:
potato (finely sliced)
turnip (finely sliced—optional)
onion (finely chopped)
4-ounce steak (chuck or skirt)
pepper and salt

Freezer Storage Life: up to 3 months

Preparation for freezing:
Roll out pastry into round or rounds. Pile up the
potato on about half the pastry. Place onion on top
of potato. Cut meat into small pieces and spread
over. Season with salt and pepper. A few pieces of
turnip or potato should be placed on top to save
the meat from drying. Damp edges of pastry, fold
over in semi-circular shape and crimp edges (by
pinching the pastry with the left hand and folding
it over with the right, to form a rope-like effect
on the side of the pastry). Pack and freeze.

To serve:
Place on a baking sheet and bake at top of oven
at 425°F/Gas 7 for 10–15 minutes, reducing to
350°F/Gas 4 for a further 40–50 minutes or until
cooked through.
Serves 2

Pork and Sausage Casserole

1½-pound shoulder of pork
½-pound pork sausages
2 onions (chopped)
2 carrots (sliced)
3 sticks celery (chopped)
1 tablespoon flour
¾ pint chicken stock
2 teaspoons mint jelly
salt and pepper

Freezer Storage Life: up to 3 months

Preparation for freezing:
Cut the pork into cubes. Fry the sausages and
when fat runs out add the pork and continue
frying until lightly browned. Remove from the
pan and place in an oven-proof dish. Fry the
vegetables in the remaining fat, stir in the flour
and gradually stir in the stock. Bring to the boil,
stirring until thickened, and add remaining
ingredients. Pour the sauce and vegetables over
the meat. Cover and cook at 350°F/Gas 4 for ¾ hour.
Cool, remove excess fat, pack and freeze.

To serve:
Reheat in a casserole in the oven, or saucepan on
top of the cooker.
Serves 4

Poulet en Cocotte

2-ounce bacon rashers
1 onion (chopped)
¼-pound button mushrooms
3-pound oven-ready chicken
salt and pepper
1 teaspoon fresh thyme (chopped)
½ pint chicken stock
¼ pint dry white wine

Freezer Storage Life: up to 2 months

Preparation for freezing:
Remove rind from the bacon and cut bacon into
pieces. Place in a frying-pan and fry until fat comes
out, add onion and mushrooms and fry for a few
minutes. Place bacon and vegetables in an oven-
proof casserole and put the chicken on top (if

chicken is a bought frozen one, allow to thaw and
remove giblets etc. from the inside). Sprinkle with
salt, pepper and thyme. Pour stock and wine over
the chicken. Cover and cook at 350°F/Gas 4 for
2 hours. Cool, pack and freeze.

To serve:
Leave chicken and vegetables to thaw slightly,
then place in a casserole. Reheat in the oven for
30 minutes, or until hot throughout.
Serves 6

Coq au Vin

8 chicken joints
seasoned flour
2-ounce butter
1 tablespoon oil
½-pound shallots (peeled)
1 clove garlic (crushed)
2 tablespoons brandy
½ pint chicken stock
½ pint red wine
1 teaspoon sugar
salt and pepper

To serve:
crescents of puff pastry
Freezer Storage Life: up to 3 months

Preparation for freezing:
Coat the chicken in seasoned flour, melt the butter
and oil in a saucepan and fry the chicken until
golden brown. Drain and place in a casserole. Fry
the shallots and garlic in the remaining oil,
add the brandy and set alight. When the flames
die out add stock, wine, sugar, salt and pepper,
bring to the boil and pour over the chicken. Cover
the casserole and cook at 325°F/Gas 3 for 1 hour.
Allow to cool then pack, seal and freeze.

To serve:
Place the chicken in a casserole and reheat at
325°F/Gas 3 for 2 hours. Serve with crescents of
puff pastry.
Serves 4

Sauté Chicken Normandy

4 chicken quarters
1-ounce butter
1 tablespoon oil
1 leek (washed and finely chopped)
1 onion (chopped)
6 tablespoons cider

To serve:
¼ pint double cream
salt and pepper
Freezer Storage Life: up to 3 months

Preparation for freezing:
Dip the chicken quarters in seasoned flour. Sauté in butter and oil in a large saucepan for 30 minutes turning occasionally until golden brown. Add the leak and onion, place lid on saucepan and cook for further 15 minutes. Add cider and simmer gently for 20–30 minutes until chicken is tender. Cool, pack and freeze.

To serve:
Reheat chicken in a saucepan, when bubbling remove from heat and stir in the cream. Add seasoning to taste, heat gently but do not allow the sauce to boil.
Serves 4

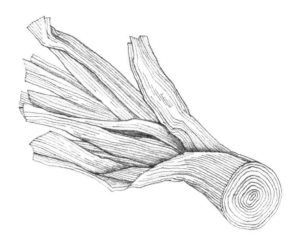

Creamed Chicken and Pimento Puffs

1-pound cooked chicken
½ pint thick white sauce
3½-ounce tin pimentos
salt and pepper
pinch paprika
13-ounce packet frozen puff pastry

To serve:
beaten egg *or* milk
Freezer Storage Life: up to 3 months

Preparation for freezing:
Cut the chicken into small pieces and mix into the sauce. Drain the pimentos, cut into strips and mix into the chicken with salt, pepper and paprika pepper. Leave in the refrigerator to firm. Roll out the pastry and cut into eight squares. Divide the chicken mixture into eight and place in the centre of each pastry square. Dampen the edges and fold over in an envelope shape. Pack and freeze.

To serve:
Place puffs on a baking tray and glaze with beaten egg or milk. Bake at 425°F/Gas 7 for 30 minutes until risen and golden brown.
Serves 4

Grouse Smitane

2 prepared grouse
3 tablespoons oil
2 onions (chopped)
2 teaspoons paprika
$\frac{1}{3}$ pint red wine
$\frac{3}{4}$ pint beef stock

Beurre manié:
1-ounce flour
1-ounce butter

salt and pepper

To serve:
$\frac{1}{4}$ pint cream
parsley (chopped)
Freezer Storage Life: up to 3 months

Preparation for freezing:
Divide each grouse into two, then fry in oil until lightly browned. Remove from the pan and place in a casserole. Add the onions, paprika, wine and stock. Cover the casserole and cook at 350°F/Gas 4 for 1 hour. Mix the flour and butter together and add it, a little at a time, to the sauce. Return the casserole to the oven and cook for a further 10 minutes, add salt and pepper to taste. Allow to cool, remove any excess fat, then pack and freeze.

To serve:
Place the grouse and sauce in a casserole and reheat at 325°F/Gas 3 for 1–1$\frac{1}{2}$ hours until hot throughout. Stir in the cream and sprinkle with chopped parsley.
Serves 4

Spareribs with Pineapple Sweet and Sour Sauce

2-pound spareribs of pork
1 onion (chopped)
1 tablespoon oil
8-ounce tin crushed pineapple
1 tablespoon demerara sugar
1 tablespoon Worcestershire sauce
juice 1 lemon
1 tablespoon vinegar
1 teaspoon made mustard
salt and pepper

Freezer Storage Life: up to 3 months

Preparation for freezing:
Place spareribs in an oven-proof dish and bake at 400°F/Gas 6 for about 40 minutes. Meanwhile fry the onion in the oil and stir in the remaining ingredients. Simmer for 10 minutes and cool. Drain the spareribs and cool. Place in a container and pour the sauce over the top. Pack and freeze.

To serve:
Reheat in the oven 325°F/Gas 3 in a covered dish for about 40 minutes, or in a saucepan on top of the cooker.
Serves 6

Duck with Cherry Sauce

2-ounce butter
2 tablespoons oil
6 joints of duck
1 large onion (chopped)
1 clove garlic (crushed)
15-ounce tin cherries
1 tablespoon lemon juice
2 tablespoons brandy
1 teaspoon sugar
salt and pepper

Freezer Storage Life: up to 3 months

Preparation for freezing:
Heat the butter and oil in a large frying- or sauce-pan. Fry the pieces of duck until golden brown, drain and transfer to an oven-proof casserole. Fry the onion and garlic for a few minutes, add remaining ingredients to the pan, bring to the boil and pour into the casserole. Cover and cook at 325°F/Gas 3, for 1 hour. Cool and remove any fat off the top. Pack and freeze.

To serve:
Reheat in the oven, 375°F/Gas 5 for 1 hour or on top of the cooker.
Serves 6

Duck with Green Peppers

1 duck (about 4-pound)
3-ounce butter
1 tablespoon oil
1 onion (chopped)
2 green peppers (deseeded and sliced)
¾ pint chicken stock
salt and pepper
1 bay leaf
pinch mixed herbs

Freezer Storage Life: up to 3 months

Preparation for freezing:
Fry the duck in the butter and oil, turning occasionally, until golden brown. Drain and place the duck in a casserole. Lightly fry the onion and peppers in remaining fat, drain and place in the casserole. Pour in the stock and add salt, pepper, bay leaf and mixed herbs. Cover the casserole and cook at 350°F/Gas 4 for 2 hours. Remove duck and divide into four portions and place in a container. Remove bay leaf from the stock and pour stock and vegetables over the duck. Allow to cool then pack and freeze.

To serve:
Place duck and sauce in a casserole and reheat at 325°F/Gas 3 for 1 hour or until hot throughout.
Serves 4

Oxtail Stew

1 oxtail (cut into pieces)
1-ounce flour
salt and pepper
1 tablespoon oil
2 onions
3 carrots
3 turnips
1 pint beef stock

To serve:
potatoes (sliced) if liked
Freezer Storage Life: up to 3 months

Preparation for freezing:
Remove excess fat from the oxtail. Mix flour with a little salt and pepper and sprinkle over the oxtail. Prepare vegetables and cut into pieces. Heat oil in a large saucepan, add the oxtail and fry until brown. Add vegetables and stock, bring to the boil, cover the pan and simmer for 2 hours until oxtail is tender. Cool and skim the fat off the top. Pack and freeze.

To serve:
Place contents in oven-proof casserole, add sliced potatoes if liked, and reheat in the oven, 325°F/Gas 3 for 1 hour or until hot throughout.
Serves 4

Herbed Sausage-Meat Pie

1 onion (chopped)
2 sticks celery (chopped)
little oil
1½-pound sausage-meat
1 teaspoon mixed herbs
salt and pepper
1 egg
12-ounce shortcrust pastry

To serve:
beaten egg *or* milk
Freezer Storage Life: up to 3 months

Preparation for freezing:
Fry the onion and celery in a little oil for a few minutes, drain and mix into the sausage-meat. Stir in the herbs, salt, pepper and beaten egg. Divide the pastry into two and roll out. Line an 8-inch pie-plate with one piece of pastry and spoon in the filling. Cover the pie with the other piece of pastry. Pack and freeze.

To serve:
Place pie on a baking tray, glaze with beaten egg or milk. Bake at 375°F/Gas 5 for 40–50 minutes.
Serves 6

Fricassée of Veal

2-pound lean veal
1 onion (chopped)
2 carrots (chopped)
3 sticks celery (chopped)
1 bay leaf
juice 1 lemon
salt and pepper
1 tablespoon cornflour
2 egg yolks

To serve:
3 tablespoons cream
seasoning (optional)
Freezer Storage Life: up to 3 months

Preparation for freezing:
Cut veal into small cubes and place in a saucepan. Add the vegetables, bay leaf, lemon juice and seasonings, cover with cold water, bring to the boil. Reduce heat, cover the pan and simmer for about 1 hour, until meat is tender. Strain off the stock and measure $\frac{3}{4}$ pint into a clean pan. Bring to the boil and thicken with the cornflour blended with a little cold water. Beat in the egg yolks and cook, stirring all the time, for 2–3 minutes. Mix sauce into the meat and vegetables. Cool, pack and freeze.

To serve:
Place the fricassée into a saucepan and bring gently to the boil, stir in the cream and add more seasoning if liked.
Serves 4–6

Prepared vegetable dishes using home grown, market garden or commercially frozen vegetables make delicious, light and nourishing lunches or suppers followed by cheese and fruit. Some of the recipes in this section such as corn fritters, stuffed potatoes, and ratatouille that take a little time to prepare also make unusual and attractive accompaniments to main dishes. An alternative way of freezing and storing vegetables is to purée them first. The vegetables should be prepared and cooked in the usual way, then blended in a liquidiser and, when cool, packed and frozen. These form an ideal basis for soups or, with the addition of an egg when reheating, a nourishing meal for babies.

Vegetables

Ratatouille

Ratatouille

2 onions (peeled and chopped)
4 tablespoons oil
2 green peppers (deseeded and sliced)
1 clove garlic (crushed)
1-pound tomatoes (skinned and sliced)
1-2 aubergines (sliced)
4 courgettes (sliced)
salt and pepper

Freezer Storage Life: up to 6 months

Preparation for freezing:
Fry the onions in the oil until transparent. Add the remaining vegetables, cover the pan and cook over low heat until the vegetables are just soft. Add seasoning to taste. Cool, remove any excess oil, pack and freeze.

To serve:
Turn the ratatouille into a saucepan cook over very low heat until soft, then raise heat and allow to simmer for a few minutes.
Serves 6

Green Beans Creole

2-pound green beans *or*
  2 (8-ounce) packets frozen whole French beans
1 onion (finely chopped)
1 green pepper (deseeded and sliced)
2-ounce butter
½-pound tomatoes (skinned and sliced)
1 teaspoon vinegar
1 teaspoon Tabasco sauce
salt and pepper
pinch sugar

Freezer Storage Life: up to 3 months

Preparation for freezing:
Trim fresh beans, wash and cook in boiling salted water, or cook frozen beans according to the instructions on the packet. Drain well and place in a container. Fry the onion and green pepper in butter for about 3 minutes. Add the tomatoes

and other ingredients then simmer for 5 minutes. Cool and pour over the beans. Cover, seal and freeze.

To serve:
Reheat gently in a saucepan on top of the cooker or in a casserole in the oven.
Serves 4

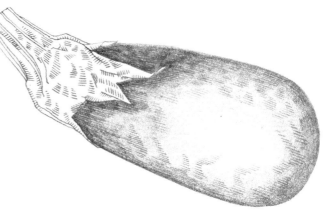

Mixed Vegetable Lyonnaise

2 onions (sliced)
2-ounce butter
1-ounce flour
¾ pint milk
3½-ounce tin pimentos
salt and pepper
2-pound cooked mixed vegetables (carrots, celery, turnip, etc.)

To serve:
1 packet potato crisps
Freezer Storage Life: up to 3 months

Preparation for freezing:
Fry the onions in butter until soft. Stir in the flour, then gradually stir in the milk and cook until thick. Drain pimentos, chop and add to the sauce with salt and pepper to taste. Dice the vegetables and place in a container, pour the sauce over the top. Cool, pack and freeze.

To serve:
Reheat in the oven 350°F/Gas 4 and when hot sprinkle the crisps over the top and bake for a further 5 minutes.
Serves 4

Vegetable Galette

1 onion (chopped)
1 tablespoon oil
½-pound tomatoes (skinned and sliced)
8-ounce packet frozen mixed vegetables
3-ounce grated cheese
salt and pepper
13-ounce packet frozen puff pastry (thawed)

Freezer Storage Life: up to 4 months

Preparation for freezing:
Fry the onion in the oil until soft, add the tomatoes and mixed vegetables, cook gently until the vegetables have thawed. Allow to cool. Stir in the cheese and salt and pepper. Roll out the pastry to a rectangle and cut in half. Place the vegetable mixture on one piece of pastry, dampen the edge with cold water and place the other piece of pastry on top. Press the edges together and mark with a fork. Pack and freeze.

To serve:
Place the galette on a baking tray and brush with beaten egg or milk. Bake at 425°F/Gas 7 for ¾–1 hour. Serve with a cheese sauce (page 57) if liked.
Serves 4

Tomato and Cauliflower Niçoise

1 onion (peeled and chopped)
1 clove garlic (crushed)
2 tablespoons oil
14-ounce tin tomatoes
¼ pint chicken stock
salt and pepper
8-12 black olives
1 cauliflower

Freezer Storage Life: up to 3 months

Preparation for freezing:
Fry the onion and garlic in the oil until soft. Add tomatoes, stock, salt, pepper and olives, cover the saucepan and simmer for about 10 minutes. Meanwhile divide the cauliflower into sprigs, wash well, and par-cook in boiling salted water, drain well. Place cauliflower in a container and pour the sauce over the top. Allow to cool, pack and freeze.

To serve:
Reheat gently in a saucepan on top of the cooker or in a casserole in the oven.
Serves 4

Potato Soufflé

2-pound potatoes
2-ounce butter
2-ounce flour
salt and pepper
4 eggs

Freezer Storage life: up to 6 months

Preparation for freezing:
Peel, slice and cook the potatoes until soft. Drain well and mash with the butter. Stir in the flour, salt and pepper. Separate the eggs and beat the yolks into the potato mixture. Whip the egg whites until stiff and fold into the soufflé. Spoon the mixture into a greased 2-pint soufflé dish or foil container. Cover, seal and freeze.

To serve:
Allow the soufflé to soften for about 1½–2 hours. Remove the cover and bake at 350°F/Gas 4 for 30 minutes then raise heat to 400°F/Gas 6 for a further 30–40 minutes until risen and golden.
Serves 4

Spinach Gratinée

½-pound tagliatelle
1 small onion (finely chopped)
2-ounce butter
2 (8-ounce) packets frozen leaf spinach
salt and pepper
4-ounce grated cheese

To serve:
1-ounce white breadcrumbs
little butter
Freezer Storage Life: up to 2 months

Preparation for freezing:
Cook the tagliatelle in boiling salted water for about 5 minutes, drain well. Fry the onion in the butter, then add the spinach and cook over low heat until spinach is thawed. Add salt and pepper to taste. Arrange layers of the tagliatelle, spinach and cheese in an individual dish. Cover, seal and freeze.

To serve:
Spread a little butter over each and sprinkle with breadcrumbs. Reheat in the oven, 350°F/Gas 4 for 20 minutes, then place under a hot grill to brown the crumbs.
Serves 4

Above, also shows Stuffed Potatoes, recipe see page 96

Corn Fritters

4-ounce plain flour
pinch salt
2 eggs
milk to mix
6-ounce packet frozen sweetcorn (thawed)

Freezer Storage Life: up to 6 months

Preparation for freezing:
Sieve the flour and salt into a basin, add the lightly beaten eggs and enough milk to make a fairly stiff batter. Stir in the sweetcorn. Fry small spoonfuls of the mixture in a greased frying pan till golden brown. Drain and cool. Pack in flat cartons with a layer of greaseproof paper between. Seal and freeze.

To serve:
Remove fritters from carton and place on a baking tray. Reheat in the oven 350°F/Gas 4 for about 20 minutes.
Serve with fried chicken or on their own with a cheese sauce (see page 57).
Serves 4

Artichokes with Mushroom and Cheese

14-ounce tin artichoke hearts
4-ounce mushrooms (sliced)
1-ounce butter
4-ounce grated Cheddar cheese
salt and pepper
2 tablespoons double cream

Freezer Storage Life: up to 3 months

Preparation for freezing:
Drain the artichoke hearts and place on a tray.
Lightly fry the mushrooms in the butter and stir
in 3 ounces of the cheese. Add salt and pepper, then
mix in the cream. Fill the centres of the artichokes
with the mushroom and cheese mixture and
sprinkle each with the remaining cheese. Place
in the freezer until hard, then remove from the
tray and pack, seal and freeze.

To serve:
Place the filled artichokes on a baking tray, cover
with foil. Bake at 350°F/Gas 4 for 20 minutes or
until hot. Remove foil and bake for a further few
minutes until cheese is golden brown.
Serves 4

Creamed Peas and Mushrooms

16-ounce packet frozen peas
4 rashers bacon (de-rinded and chopped)
$\frac{1}{4}$-pound mushrooms (chopped)
pinch mixed herbs
$\frac{1}{4}$ pint double cream

To serve:
fried bread triangles
Freezer Storage Life: up to 2 months

Preparation for freezing:
Par-cook the peas in boiling salted water for about
3 minutes. Fry the bacon and mushrooms and add
the herbs. Drain peas and stir in the bacon and
mushrooms. Allow to cool then stir in the cream.
Pack and freeze.

To serve:
Reheat gently either in a saucepan on top of the
cooker or in a casserole in the oven. Serve garnished with triangles of fried bread.
Serves 4

Cheese and Onion Savoury

2 onions (peeled and chopped)
4-ounce white breadcrumbs
1 pint milk
3 eggs
6-ounce grated cheese
salt and pepper

Freezer Storage Life: up to 6 months

Preparation for freezing:
Cook the onions in boiling salted water until soft, then drain. Mix breadcrumbs with the milk, separate eggs and beat the yolks into the breadcrumb mixture. Leave aside for at least 10 minutes. Beat the egg whites until stiff. Add the onions, cheese, salt and pepper to the breadcrumb mixture and fold in the egg whites. Spoon into greased individual foil dishes, cover, seal and freeze.

To serve:
Allow to soften for about 15–30 minutes, remove covers and place the dishes on a baking tray. Bake at 350°F/Gas 4 for 30–40 minutes until risen and golden brown.
Serves 6

Cauliflower Gruyère

1 cauliflower
1 pint béchamel sauce (page 57)
4-ounce Gruyère cheese (sliced)
cayenne pepper

Freezer Storage Life: up to 3 months

Preparation for freezing:
Separate the cauliflower into sprigs and wash well in salted water. Cook the cauliflower in boiling salted water until partly cooked. Drain well and place in a large dish (or 4 individual dishes). Pour the sauce over the cauliflower and arrange slices of the cheese on top. Sprinkle with a little cayenne pepper. Pack and freeze.

To serve:
Place in the oven, 350°F/Gas 4, for 1–1¼ hours until cheese has melted and is hot throughout.
Serves 4

Stuffed Potatoes

4 large potatoes
1 onion (peeled and chopped)
1 tablespoon oil
3 rashers bacon
1 teaspoon made mustard
salt and pepper
1 egg

To serve:
2-ounce grated cheese
Freezer Storage Life: up to 3 months

Preparation for freezing:
Wash the potatoes and bake in the oven (400°F/Gas 6) for 1–1½ hours or until cooked. Halve and scoop out the centres.
Meanwhile cut the bacon into pieces and fry. When the fat begins to run out add the onions and fry until soft. Mash the potatoes, add the bacon, onion, mustard, salt, pepper and the egg and mix well.
Return the potato mixture to the skins. Wrap in freezer foil, seal and freeze.

To serve:
Place the foil wrapped potatoes in the oven 350°F/Gas 4 and reheat for ¾–1 hour. Remove the foil, sprinkle top of potatoes with grated cheese and place under the grill to melt the cheese.
Serves 4

Like the starter to a meal, the last course—a dessert—can be served either hot or cold and should complement the first parts of the meal. With a freezer, one can provide a wide variety of desserts. Mousse, sorbet and ice-creams, for which recipes are given, can be made with different fruits and flavourings. Basic recipes such as babas and pancakes only need to be finished off before serving and the puddings that are usually served hot merely require heating through and decoration.

Desserts, hot and cold

Milanese Soufflé
Coffee Ice-Cream
Swiss Fruit Flan

Milanese Soufflé

3 eggs
3-ounce caster sugar
grated rind of 1 and juice of 2 lemons
½-ounce gelatine
2 tablespoons hot water
½ pint double cream
1-ounce chopped nuts (toasted)

Freezer Storage Life: up to 4 months

Preparation for freezing:
Separate the eggs and place yolks, sugar and lemon juice in a basin over a saucepan of boiling water. Whisk over heat until the mixture is thick and creamy. Add grated lemon rind and leave to cool. Dissolve gelatine in the hot water and add to the lemon mixture. Whip the cream and fold into the mixture. Whisk egg whites until stiff and fold into the soufflé.

Tie a double piece of greaseproof paper around a 1-pint soufflé dish to project 1½ inches above the rim. Pour the soufflé into the dish. Place in the freezer until set, then remove the paper. Press the chopped nuts around the edge of the soufflé. Return to the freezer to harden then wrap and return to the freezer.

To serve:
Allow to thaw for about 3 hours at room temperature and if liked, pipe cream on the top.
Serves 6

Swiss Fruit Flan

Short-crust pastry:
6-ounce plain flour
3-ounce butter or margarine
cold water to mix

Filling:
8-ounce peaches *or* apricots
2-ounce self-raising flour
2-ounce caster sugar
2-ounce soft margarine
1 large egg
½ teaspoon almond essence
2 tablespoons peach *or* apricot jam

Freezer Storage Life: up to 3 months

Preparation for freezing:
For the short-crust pastry, place the flour and butter or margarine in a bowl and rub the fat into the flour until the mixture resembles fine breadcrumbs. Mix to firm dough with water. Roll out and line a 7-inch sandwich tin or flan ring. Trim the edges and reserve the scraps of pastry.

Stone and slice the fruit and simmer gently in a little water until soft. Strain and reserve the syrup. Cream together the margarine and caster sugar, beat in the egg and almond essence, fold in the flour.

Place the cooled fruit in the base of the pastry case and spread sponge mixture over the top. Roll out the scraps of pastry and cut into strips. Arrange these in lattice pattern over the top of the flan. Bake at 375°F/Gas 5 for 50–60 minutes until well risen and firm to touch. Meanwhile place the jam and 2 tablespoons of the syrup in a saucepan and boil for 1–2 minutes. Brush the top of the flan thickly with the glaze. Cool, pack and freeze. Freeze the reserved syrup separately.

To serve:
Leave to thaw overnight in the refrigerator or about 6 hours at room temperature. Serve either cold with cream or heat through in the oven for about 20–30 minutes and serve with custard. The remaining syrup should be served separately.
Serves 4–6

Queen's Apple Pie

$\frac{1}{2}$ pint milk
2 eggs
1$\frac{1}{2}$-pound cooking apples (peeled and sliced)
grated rind and juice 1 lemon
2-ounce sugar
4 sponge cakes

Freezer Storage Life: up to 4 months

Preparation for freezing:
Bring the milk almost to the boil. Separate the eggs and beat in a little of the warm milk to the yolks, return this to the remainder of the milk and cook over a gentle heat until the custard thickens. Remove from heat and cool. Meanwhile cook the apples with lemon rind, juice and sugar—add a little water if necessary—until the apples are soft. Cool and mix into the custard. Place the sponge cakes in an oven-proof dish and pour the apple mixture on top. Pack and freeze. Place the egg whites in a separate container and freeze separately.

To serve:
Remove the pudding from the freezer 1–2 hours before required. Thaw the egg whites then whip until stiff. Fold in the caster sugar and pile on top of the apple mixture. Bake at 350°F/Gas 4 for 15 minutes.
Serves 4–6

Walnut Fruit Crumble

3-ounce margarine
8-ounce plain flour
3-ounce demerara sugar
2-ounce chopped walnuts
2-pound fruit (apples, plums, peaches etc.) sugared
   to taste

Freezer Storage Life: up to 6 months

Preparation for freezing:
Rub the margarine into the flour, mix in the sugar and walnuts. Prepare the fruit and cook in water until just soft. Drain off excess water and add sugar to the fruit. Place fruit in an oven-proof or foil dish. Spoon the walnut mixture on top and press down lightly. Cover, seal and freeze.

To serve:
Remove wrappings, allow to soften for 1 hour and place the pudding in the oven 325°F/Gas 3 for 40 minutes until cooked.
Serves 6

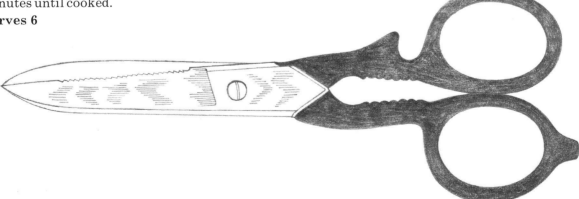

101

Redcurrant Cheesecake

4-ounce digestive biscuits
2-ounce sugar
2-ounce butter (melted)
¾-pound redcurrants
2 eggs
4-ounce caster sugar
½ teaspoon vanilla essence
½-ounce gelatine
6 tablespoons hot water
½-pound cream cheese *or* sieved cottage cheese
¼ pint double cream

Freezer Storage Life: up to 3 months

Preparation for freezing:
Crush the biscuits and mix with sugar and melted butter. Press the crumb mixture over the base of a 7-inch loose-based cake-tin. Prepare the redcurrants and cook over a low heat until soft. Cool and put through an electric blender, or sieve, to make a purée. Separate the eggs and beat yolks and sugar together until creamy. Stir in the vanilla essence and cheese, mix until evenly blended. Dissolve the gelatine in hot water and add to the cheese mixture with the redcurrant purée. Stir well and leave in a cool place until beginning to set. Whip the egg whites until stiff. Fold cream and egg whites into the mixture and pour into the tin. Leave to set. Remove the cheesecake from the tin and put on to a plate. Place in the freezer until hard, then pack and return to the freezer.

To serve:
Allow to thaw for 6–8 hours or overnight in the refrigerator. Decorate with whipped cream and chopped nuts.
Serves 4

Apple Puff Strudel

Pancakes

4-ounce plain flour
pinch salt
1 egg
½ pint milk
½-ounce butter (melted)

Freezer Storage Life: up to 3 months

Preparation for freezing:
Sieve flour and salt into a basin, add the egg, milk and butter. Beat well until smooth and creamy. Pour a little of the batter into an oiled 7-inch frying-pan; tilt the pan so that the batter covers the base. Fry on both sides until golden brown. Continue until all the batter is cooked.
Leave the pancakes to cool, then pack in layers with a piece of greaseproof paper between each one. Wrap and freeze.

To serve:
Allow pancakes to thaw out for about 15 minutes. If required hot, place in a shallow oven-proof dish, cover with foil and heat in the oven for 10 minutes. Serve with lemon and sugar or spread with golden syrup, roll up and sprinkle with icing sugar.
Note: pancakes can also have a savoury filling, cheese, ham and mushroom or fish, then covered with a sauce and reheated in the oven.
Serves 4

Apple Puff Strudel

2 cooking apples (peeled and chopped)
1 tablespoon lemon juice
2-ounce raisins
2-ounce currants
2-ounce demerara sugar
1 teaspoon mixed spice
7½-ounce packet frozen puff pastry (thawed)
1-ounce butter (softened)

Freezer Storage Life: up to 4 months

Preparation for freezing:
Mix apples, lemon juice, raisins and currants, sugar and spice together. Roll out the pastry, thinly to a square, and spread with the butter. Place apple filling on the pastry, leaving about ½ inch around the edges. Brush edges with water then form into a roll. Pack and freeze.

To serve:
Remove the pastry roll from the packing and place on a baking tray. If frozen, bake at 425°F/Gas 7 for 40–45 minutes; if thawed, for 25–30 minutes. Sprinkle with caster sugar.
Serves 4–6

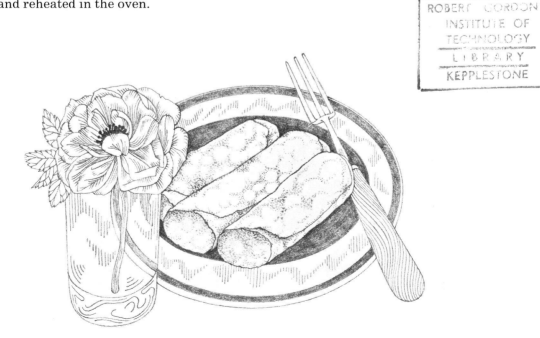

Lemon Sorbet

grated rind of 1 and juice of 2 lemons
cold water
2-ounce caster sugar
1 teaspoon gelatine
2 egg whites

Freezer Storage Life: up to 6 months

Preparation for freezing:
Mix rind and lemon juice and make up to $1\frac{1}{4}$ pints with cold water. Bring this to the boil with the sugar and stir in the gelatine. Leave to cool then place in the freezer and leave until almost hard. Whisk egg whites and beat into the lemon mixture. Place in containers, cover and freeze.

To serve:
Remove from freezer about $\frac{1}{2}$ hour before required.
Serves 6

Variations
Orange: Use the juice of 3 oranges or a can of frozen orange juice with grated rind of 1 orange.

Raspberry, strawberry and other fruits: Use $\frac{1}{2}$ pint fruit purée instead of the lemon or orange rind and juice.

Vanilla Ice-Cream

$\frac{1}{2}$ pint milk
3 egg yolks
2-ounce caster sugar
2-3 drops vanilla essence
$\frac{1}{2}$ pint double cream *or* evaporated milk (whipped)

Freezer Storage Life: up to 6 months

Preparation for freezing:
Bring the milk almost to the boil. Mix egg yolks with the sugar and vanilla essence and stir in the milk. Strain back into the saucepan and cook over low heat until the mixture just coats the back of the spoon. Pour into a basin and place in the freezer. Leave until the mixture is almost frozen. Whisk well and beat in the whipped cream. Spoon into a container, cover and freeze.

To serve:
Allow to soften slightly for about 10 minutes before eating.
Serves 6

Variations
Chocolate: Add 2-ounce melted plain chocolate to the warmed milk.

Coffee: Add 1–2 tablespoons coffee essence to the mixture when beating before adding the cream.

Raspberry: Add $\frac{1}{2}$ pint raspberry purée to the custard instead of the cream.

Strawberry: As above.

Almond Pudding

4-ounce butter
8-ounce caster sugar
1-pound cream cheese
4 eggs
4-ounce semolina
4-ounce ground almonds
grated rind and juice 1 lemon
4-ounce raisins
4 drops almond essence

Freezer Storage Life: up to 3 months

Preparation for freezing:
Cream the butter and sugar until light and fluffy, then beat in the cream cheese. Separate the eggs and beat the yolks into the creamed mixture. Stir in the semolina, ground almonds, lemon rind, juice, raisins and almond essence. Beat the egg whites until stiff and fold into the mixture. Spoon into a greased 8-inch cake-tin and bake at 350°F/ Gas 4 for 45 minutes until firm. Leave to cool slightly then turn out of the tin. When cold pack and freeze.

To serve:
Leave to thaw overnight in the refrigerator or 3–4 hours at room temperature.
Serves 6–8

Bakewell Tart

6-ounce short-crust pastry
jam
2-ounce margarine
2-ounce caster sugar
1 egg
$\frac{1}{4}$ teaspoon vanilla essence
$\frac{1}{2}$ teaspoon almond essence
1-ounce ground almonds
$1\frac{1}{2}$-ounce cakecrumbs

Freezer Storage Life: up to 6 months

Preparation for freezing:
Grease a 7-inch sandwich-tin.
Roll out the pastry and line the prepared tin. Trim case and reserve the pastry. Spread a little jam on the base. Cream the margarine until light and fluffy and beat in the egg. Stir in the essences, ground almonds and cakecrumbs and mix well. Spoon this mixture into the pastry case. Roll out pastry trimmings and cut into thin strips, twist and place on top of the tart, to form a lattice.
Bake at 350°F/Gas 4 for 35–40 minutes. Cool in the tin, then turn out, wrap and freeze.

To serve:
Allow to thaw out at room temperature for 3–4 hours. Cut into thin wedges and sprinkle with icing sugar.

Chocolate Freezer Gâteau

42 sponge finger biscuits
8-ounce plain chocolate
3 tablespoons water
2-3 drops vanilla essence
2 eggs
2 tablespoons icing sugar
½ pint double cream

Freezer Storage Life: up to 3 months

Preparation for freezing:
Line a 2-pound loaf-tin (or 2-pint soufflé-dish) with a double layer of greaseproof paper. Arrange a layer of sponge fingers on the base and around the sides of the tin or dish.
Melt the chocolate in a basin over a saucepan of hot water. Add the water and vanilla essence and remove from the heat. Separate the eggs, and beat the yolks into the chocolate with the icing sugar. Whip the cream until almost thick and beat the egg whites. Stir the cream into the chocolate mixture and fold in the egg whites. Pour ⅓ of the chocolate into the tin, cover with a layer of sponge fingers. Repeat twice with remaining mixture and sponge fingers.
Place in the freezer until hard. Remove from the tin or dish, pack and return to the freezer.

To serve:
Allow to thaw out at room temperature for 3–4 hours. Remove wrapping and greaseproof paper. Decorate with whipped cream and grated chocolate.
Serves 6–8

Raspberry Mousse

1-pound fresh raspberries (or 2 15-ounce tins, drained)
½-ounce gelatine
¼ pint hot water
sugar to taste
2 egg whites

Freezer Storage Life: up to 3 months

Preparation for freezing:
Put the raspberries through an electric blender or mash well with a fork. Dissolve the gelatine in hot water and leave to cool. Mix gelatine with the raspberries and add sugar to taste. Leave until almost set. Beat the egg whites and fold into the raspberry mixture. Spoon into 1 large or 4 individual containers. Cover and freeze.

To serve:
Leave to thaw overnight in the refrigerator or 2–3 hours at room temperature.
Serves 4
Note: This mousse can be made with other soft fruits instead.

Bread and Butter Pudding

6 slices white bread
butter
3-ounce currants
3 eggs
pinch nutmeg
2-ounce caster sugar
1 pint milk

Freezer Storage Life: up to 3 months

Preparation for freezing:
Spread the slices of bread with butter and cut into fingers. Place in a 2-pint pie-dish with layers of currants. Beat eggs, nutmeg and sugar together, add the milk and strain on to the bread. Leave aside for 15 minutes. Pack and freeze.

To serve:
Leave to thaw for 6–8 hours, then bake at 325°F/Gas 3 for 45 minutes, until firm and golden.
Serves 4–6

Plum Sponge Pudding

1½-pound plums
2-ounce sugar
½ teaspoon cinnamon
2-ounce margarine
2-ounce caster sugar
1 egg
3-ounce self-raising flour
little warm water

Freezer Storage Life: up to 3 months

Preparation for freezing:
Wash the plums and cook in a little water until soft. Drain off excess water, mix sugar and cinnamon with the plums and put into a pie-dish. Cream the margarine and sugar and when soft and creamy beat in the egg. Fold in the flour and add 1–2 tablespoons warm water to give a soft consistency. Spread the cake mixture over the plums and bake at 350°F/Gas 4 for 30 minutes. Cool, pack and freeze.

To serve:
Cold: leave to thaw for 6–8 hours.
Hot: leave to soften slightly for about an hour, then reheat in the oven 325°F/Gas 3.
Serves 4

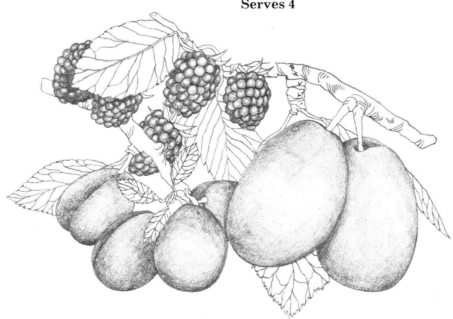

Most cakes, biscuits, scones and breads freeze extremely well and it is well worth while when you have a baking session to make extra quantities to freeze. Although the basic mixtures can be frozen before baking, better results are obtained if they are cooked first—it also saves time as all you have to do is allow the cake or bread to thaw before decorating and serving it. If large, rich cakes are frozen, it is a good idea to divide them into portions before wrapping, then if only two or three pieces are required it saves waiting until the whole cake has thawed. Cakes that have a butter-cream frosting should be put into the freezer to harden and then wrapped, as this prevents the cream being squashed.

Baking for the Freezer

Selection of Sweet Biscuits
Lemon Chiffon Cake
Bridge Rolls

Almond Biscuits

4-ounce butter
5-ounce caster sugar
1 egg
4-ounce plain flour
1 teaspoon baking powder
1 teaspoon almond essence
3-ounce chopped almonds

Freezer Storage Life: up to 6 months

Preparation for freezing:
Cream the butter and sugar until light and fluffy. Beat in the egg then stir in the flour and other ingredients. Place small spoonfuls of the mixture (about the size of a walnut) on greased baking trays. Bake at 400°F/Gas 6 for 8 minutes. Cool on a wire rack, pack and freeze.

To serve:
Allow to thaw out for 2–3 hours.

Gingernuts

8-ounce self-raising flour
2 teaspoons ground ginger
$\frac{1}{2}$ teaspoon mixed spice
3-ounce butter
2-ounce caster sugar
2 tablespoons treacle
2-3 teaspoons milk

Freezer Storage Life: up to 6 months

Preparation for freezing:
Sieve the flour, ginger and mixed spice into a basin. Rub in the butter and add the sugar. Warm the treacle and milk slightly and add to the dry ingredients to make a firm dough. Roll out on a floured board to about $\frac{1}{4}$-inch thick and cut into rounds with a 2-inch cutter. Place on a greased baking-tray and bake at 375°F/Gas 5 for 10–12 minutes. Cool on a wire rack, wrap and freeze.

To serve:
Allow to thaw out for about an hour at room temperature.

Chocolate Shells

3-ounce butter
2-ounce icing sugar
2-3 drops vanilla essence
2-ounce plain chocolate (melted)
2-ounce cornflour
3-ounce plain flour

Filling:
2-ounce butter
2-ounce icing sugar
1 tablespoon cocoa
few drops peppermint essence
1 tablespoon double cream

Freezer Storage Life: up to 6 months

Preparation for freezing:
Cream butter with the icing sugar and vanilla essence until light and fluffy. Stir in the chocolate and mix well, then stir in the sieved cornflour and flour. Put the mixture into a piping bag with a shell tube. Pipe 'shells' on to baking trays. Bake at 350°F/Gas 4 for 10–15 minutes, cool on wire trays.

For the filling:
Cream butter and icing sugar together then beat in the other ingredients. Sandwich 2 'shells' together with the filling. Pack and freeze.

To serve:
Allow to thaw out for 1–2 hours.

Florentines

½-ounce glacé cherries (chopped)
1½-ounce mixed peel
4-ounce blanched almonds (chopped)
2-ounce butter
2-ounce caster sugar
1 tablespoon honey
1 tablespoon double cream
4-ounce plain chocolate

Freezer Storage Life: up to 6 months

Preparation for freezing:
Place the cherries, mixed peel and almonds in a saucepan. Add the butter, sugar, honey and cream and stir over gentle heat until mixed together. Spread the mixture on to a well-greased baking-tray. Bake at 350°F/Gas 4 for 6–8 minutes until set and light golden brown. Cut into 2-inch squares, cool slightly, remove from the baking-tray and cool. Melt the chocolate in a basin over a saucepan of hot water. Coat the bases of the florentines with the chocolate and when almost set mark with a fork to make ripples. When chocolate is set, wrap and freeze.
To serve:
Allow to thaw out at room temperature for about 1 hour.

Viennese Whirls

3-ounce butter
1-ounce icing sugar
3-ounce plain flour
pinch salt

Freezer Storage Life: up to 6 months

Preparation for freezing:
Cream the butter and icing sugar together. Sieve flour and salt and beat into the creamed mixture. Put a 1-inch star pipe into a piping bag and place the biscuit mixture in this. Pipe stars about 1½ inches wide on to a baking-tray. Bake at 425°F/Gas 7 for 8–10 minutes. Cool, wrap and freeze.
To serve:
Allow to thaw out at room temperature and serve plain or sandwiched together with butter icing.

Coffee Biscuits

8-ounce butter
2-ounce icing sugar
1 tablespoon instant coffee
6-ounce plain flour
2-ounce cornflour

Freezer Storage Life: up to 6 months

Preparation for freezing:
Cream the butter and sugar until light and fluffy. Dissolve the coffee in 1 teaspoon water and stir into the creamed mixture. Stir in the flour and cornflour and work together until smooth. Spoon the mixture into a piping bag with a plain nozzle and pipe either rounds or fingers on to baking-trays. Chill for 10 minutes. Bake at 375°F/Gas 5 for 15 minutes. Cool on rack, then wrap and freeze.
To serve:
Allow to thaw out for about an hour. If liked the biscuits can be coated with coffee glacé icing.

Jam Layer Fingers

12-ounce self-raising flour
6-ounce margarine
grated rind 1 lemon
3-ounce caster sugar
2 eggs
little milk, if necessary
raspberry jam

Freezer Storage Life: up to 6 months

Preparation for freezing:
Grease an 11 × 7-inch rectangular tin.
Rub the margarine into the flour, add the lemon rind and sugar. Lightly beat the eggs and stir into the dry ingredients, add a little milk if necessary, to make a soft but manageable dough. Divide the mixture into 2 and roll out each piece the size of the tin. Place one piece in the tin and spread with jam, place the other piece on top. Brush with a little milk and sprinkle with sugar. Bake at 375°F/Gas 5 for 20–25 minutes until firm and golden. Cut into fingers, then remove from tin and cool. Wrap and freeze.
To serve:
Allow to thaw out at room temperature for 1–2 hours.

Date and Walnut Loaf

½-pound self-raising flour
pinch salt
4-ounce margarine
4-ounce soft brown sugar
8-ounce chopped dates
2-ounce chopped walnuts
2 eggs (beaten)
¼ pint milk
few drops vanilla essence

Freezer Storage Life: up to 6 months

Preparation for freezing:
Grease and line a 1½-pound loaf-tin.
Sieve flour and salt into a basin, rub in the margarine until the mixture resembles fine bread-crumbs. Add sugar, dates and walnuts, and beat in eggs, milk and vanilla essence.
Spoon the mixture into the prepared tin and bake at 350°F/Gas 4 for 1–1½ hours.
Turn out on to a cooling-rack. When cold, wrap and freeze.
To serve:
Allow the cake to thaw out for about 4 hours at room temperature.

Sachertorte

8 eggs+2 egg whites
6-ounce melted chocolate
4-ounce unsalted butter (softened)
1 teaspoon vanilla essence
pinch salt
6-ounce caster sugar
4-ounce plain flour

Filling:
apricot jam

Glaze:
4-ounce plain chocolate
½ pint double cream
4-ounce caster sugar
1 egg

Freezer Storage Life: up to 3 months

Preparation for freezing:
Grease and line 2–9-inch sandwich-tins.
Separate the eggs, place yolks in one basin and whites in another. Lightly beat the yolks then beat in the melted chocolate and softened butter. Add vanilla essence. Whisk the egg whites with the salt until stiff, and fold in the sugar. Add the whisked egg whites to the chocolate mixture and fold in the flour. Pour into the prepared tins and bake at 350°F/Gas 4 for 25 minutes. Turn out and cool on wire racks.
For the glaze:
Place chocolate, cream and sugar in a heavy-based saucepan, cook over low heat until sugar is dissolved. Raise heat and cook for another 5 minutes (or until a drop poured into cold water forms a soft ball). Leave to cool. Beat the egg and stir in 4 tablespoons of the chocolate mixture and blend well. Pour on to remaining chocolate in the pan and cook gently until the mixture coats the back of a spoon, remove from heat and cool. Sandwich the cakes with apricot jam and pour the glaze over the top and sides of the cake. When set, place in freezer to harden then wrap and freeze.
To serve:
Allow cake to thaw out for about 4 hours at room temperature.

Hazelnut Triangles

4-ounce butter
8-ounce plain flour
2-ounce caster sugar
1 egg

Topping:
3-ounce butter
3-ounce caster sugar
2-3 drops vanilla essence
2-ounce hazelnuts (finely chopped)
1 egg yolk

Freezer Storage Life: up to 6 months

Preparation for freezing:
Grease an 8-inch sandwich-tin. Rub the butter into the flour, add the sugar and mix to a firm dough with the egg. Roll out to fit the tin, and place the dough in the tin. Bake at 350°F/Gas 4 for 30 minutes.
For the topping: Cream the butter with the sugar until light and fluffy. Beat in the vanilla essence, hazelnuts and egg yolk. Spread this on the half-baked dough and return to the oven for a further 15 minutes. Divide into 8 triangles and leave to cool. Wrap and freeze.

To serve:
Allow to thaw out for about 3 hours and sprinkle with icing sugar.

Swiss Roll

2 eggs
2-ounce caster sugar
2-ounce plain flour
pinch salt
tablespoon warm water
raspberry (or other) jam

Freezer Storage Life: up to 6 months

Preparation for freezing:
Grease and flour a $7\frac{1}{2} \times 11\frac{1}{2}$-inch swiss roll tin. Make the cake as for sponge sandwich, (page 121). Spoon into the prepared tin and bake at 400°F/Gas 6 for 12–14 minutes.
To roll: place a piece of greaseproof paper slightly larger than the cake on to a clean damp cloth. Sprinkle the paper with caster sugar, then turn out the cake on to this. Using the paper as a guide, roll up the sponge (leaving the paper in the roll). Leave until almost cool then unroll the sponge, remove paper, and spread the cake with jam then re-roll. Wrap and freeze.
To serve:
Leave to thaw at room temperature for 2 hours; sprinkle with caster sugar.

Note: sponge sandwiches and swiss rolls can be varied by adding flavourings.

Chocolate: substitute $\frac{1}{2}$ ounce cocoa for $\frac{1}{2}$ ounce of the flour.

Coffee: dissolve $1\frac{1}{2}$ teaspoons instant coffee in the warm water.

Orange or **lemon:** add the grated rind of orange or lemon to the flour.

Melting Moments

4-ounce margarine
4-ounce lard
6-ounce caster sugar
9-ounce plain flour
1 teaspoon baking powder
1 egg
porridge oats

Freezer Storage Life: up to 6 months

Preparation for freezing:
Cream the fats with the sugar. Sieve flour and baking powder and mix into the creamed mixture with the egg. Mix well to form a smooth dough. Form into a roll and cut into small pieces. Make into small balls with wet hands and toss in the porridge oats. Place on baking-trays, flatten slightly with a fork. Bake at 350°F/Gas 4 for 20–25 minutes. Cool on a wire rack. Wrap and freeze.
To serve:
Allow to thaw out at room temperature for about 1 hour.

Shortbread

5-ounce plain flour
1-ounce rice flour
1 teaspoon salt
2-ounce caster sugar
4-ounce butter

Freezer Storage Life: up to 6 months

Preparation for freezing:
Sieve flour, rice, flour and salt into a basin. Add the sugar. Rub in the butter and knead until a soft dough is formed. Turn on to a floured board and knead until smooth. Press into a 7-inch sandwich-tin and smooth the top with a palette knife. Crimp the edges with a fork and mark into 6 triangles.
Bake at 300°F/Gas 2 for 1–1¼ hours. Sprinkle with caster sugar and when cold cut into 6 pieces. Wrap and freeze.
To serve:
Allow to thaw out for about 2 hours at room temperature.

Chelsea Buns

½-ounce fresh *or* ¼-ounce dried yeast
¼ pint milk
1 teaspoon sugar
8-ounce plain flour
pinch salt
1-ounce margarine
1-ounce butter, melted
4-ounce currants
2-ounce sugar
½ teaspoon mixed spice

Freezer Storage Life: up to 3 months

Preparation for freezing:
Dissolve the fresh yeast in the milk and sugar or sprinkle the dried yeast on to the milk and sugar and leave for 10 minutes until frothy. Sieve the flour and salt and rub in the margarine. Add the yeast liquid to make a soft dough (if necessary add a little more milk). Knead well, cover with a piece of oiled polythene and leave to double in size.
Knead again and roll the dough out to a 10-inch square. Brush with the melted butter and sprinkle the currants, sugar and spice over the top. Roll up like a swiss roll and cut into 9 slices. Place these on a greased baking-tray, cover with oiled polythene and leave to rise for 20 minutes. Bake at 425°F/Gas 7 for about 20 minutes. While still hot brush with a sugar glaze, made by dissolving 2 tablespoons sugar in hot water.
Cool, wrap and freeze.

To serve:
Allow to thaw out at room temperature for 2-3 hours or over-night in the refrigerator.

Chocolate Honey Cake

6-ounce butter
3-ounce demerara sugar
3-ounce clear honey
3 eggs
4½-ounce self-raising flour
pinch salt
1½-ounce cocoa
1 teaspoon coffee essence
few drops vanilla essence

Icing:
4-ounce butter
8-ounce icing sugar
2-ounce melted chocolate

Freezer Storage Life: up to 6 months

Preparation for freezing:
Grease and flour 2-7-inch sandwich-tins.
Cream butter, sugar and honey together. Lightly beat the eggs and beat into the creamed mixture. Sieve flour, salt and cocoa together and fold into the creamed mixture. Stir in coffee essence and vanilla essence. Spoon into the prepared tin and bake at 350°F/Gas 4 for 30–40 minutes. Turn out and cool.
For icing:
Cream butter and icing sugar until light and fluffy and beat in the melted chocolate.
Sandwich the cakes with half the icing and swirl the remainder over the top of the cake. Then wrap and freeze.
To serve:
Allow cake to thaw out for at least 4 hours.

Genoese Cake

4 eggs
4-ounce caster sugar
4-ounce plain flour
pinch salt
1-ounce melted butter

Freezer Storage Life: up to 6 months

Preparation for freezing:
Grease and flour 2-7-inch sandwich-tins.
Place eggs and sugar in a basin over a saucepan of hot water and whisk together until the mixture leaves a trail. Sieve the flour and salt and fold half into the whisked mixture, gently stir in half the melted butter. Repeat, adding the rest of the flour and butter. Spoon into the prepared tins and bake at 400°F/Gas 6 for 18–20 minutes. Turn out and cool on wire racks.
If liked, fill with butter icing (chocolate, coffee, orange or lemon flavoured). Place in freezer until hard then wrap and freeze.
To serve:
Allow to thaw out at room temperature for about 3 hours.
Note: this cake makes an ideal basis for iced fancies. Cut the cake into various shapes and coat with glacé icing. Wrap as above.

Gingerbread

8-ounce soft brown sugar
6-ounce butter
12-ounce golden syrup
1-pound plain flour
1 teaspoon salt
1 tablespoon ground ginger
2 teaspoons baking powder
1 egg
½ pint milk

Freezer Storage Life: up to 6 months

Preparation for freezing:
Grease and line a 2-pound loaf-tin.
Melt the sugar, butter and syrup in a saucepan over gentle heat until the sugar is dissolved. Leave to cool. Sieve the dry ingredients into a basin, make a well in the centre and stir in the melted mixture, egg and milk. Beat well to a smooth consistency. Pour into the prepared tin and bake at 325°F/Gas 3 for 1¼–1½ hours. Turn out and cool on a wire rack. Wrap and freeze.
To serve:
Allow to thaw out for about 4 hours.

Streusel Cake

3-ounce margarine
6-ounce caster sugar
1 egg
6-ounce self-raising flour
pinch salt
¼ pint milk

Topping:
3-ounce soft brown sugar
1-ounce margarine (melted)
1-ounce self-raising flour
1 teaspoon cinnamon
2-ounce chopped walnuts

Freezer Storage Life: up to 6 months

Preparation for freezing:
Grease a 7 × 11 × 1-inch deep tin.
Cream the margarine and sugar together until
light and fluffy, then beat in the egg. Sieve flour
and salt together and stir into the creamed
mixture with the milk.
For the topping:
Mix the sugar with the margarine and stir in the
flour, cinnamon and walnuts.
Spoon half the cake mixture into the prepared tin,
sprinkle with half the topping. Cover with remaining cake mixture and sprinkle with the rest of
the topping. Bake at 350°F/Gas 4 for 35–40
minutes. Cool on a wire rack. Wrap and freeze.

To serve:
Allow cake to thaw out at room temperature for
about 3 hours.

Meringues

4 egg whites
8-ounce caster sugar

Filling:
½ pint double cream
little caster *or* icing sugar

Freezer Storage Life: up to 3 months

Preparation for freezing:
Whisk the egg whites until stiff. Fold in half the
sugar and continue whisking until the mixture
stands up in peaks. Fold in the remaining sugar.

Put the mixture into a large piping bag with a rose nozzle. Pipe the meringues on to lightly oiled baking-trays. Bake at 225°F/Gas ¼ for 3 hours or until completely dry throughout. Cool.

Whip the cream until thick and add sugar to taste. Sandwich the meringues with the cream and place on a baking-tray. Freeze and then pack the meringues in cartons with a piece of foil between each layer, cover and freeze.

To serve:
Allow to thaw out for about 1–2 hours at room temperature.

Croissants

1-ounce fresh *or* ½-ounce dried yeast
¾ pint milk and water (mixed, and warmed)
1 teaspoon sugar
1¼-pound strong flour
1 teaspoon salt
1½-ounce melted butter
8-ounce butter
beaten egg to glaze

Freezer Storage Life: up to 2 months

Preparation for freezing:
Blend the fresh yeast with the sugar and mix with the milk and water, or sprinkle the dried yeast on to the milk and water and sugar, leave for 10 minutes until frothy. Sieve the flour and salt, add the yeast liquid and melted butter. Knead lightly to form a smooth dough then leave in the refrigerator for 30 minutes. Divide the piece of butter into 3 pieces.

Roll out the dough to an oblong, approximately 21 × 7 inches, dot one piece of the butter on to ⅔ of the dough, fold the plain piece over on to half the buttered dough and fold the remaining piece on top (like an envelope). Leave in the refrigerator to cool for about 10 minutes, then continue rolling, with the butter, twice more.

Divide the dough into 4 pieces and roll each piece to an oblong 18 × 9 inches and cut into 5 triangles. Roll the triangles up, from the base to the point, and curl ends round to form a crescent. Place on greased baking-trays, cover with oiled polythene and leave to rise for 15–20 minutes. Brush each with beaten egg. Bake at 450°F/Gas 8 for 10–15 minutes. Cool, wrap and freeze.

To serve:
Place required number of croissants on a baking-tray and heat through in the oven for 5–10 minutes.

Bridge Rolls

1½-ounce fresh *or* ¾-ounce dried yeast
¼ pint milk (warmed)
1-ounce sugar
1-ounce butter
2 eggs
1-pound strong flour
1 teaspoon salt
egg and salt to glaze

Freezer Storage Life: up to 3 months

Preparation for freezing:
Add the yeast to half the warmed milk and sugar and mix well, or sprinkle the dried yeast on to half the milk and sugar and leave until frothy.

Melt the butter in the remaining milk and beat in the eggs. Sieve the flour and salt and stir in the yeast and egg mixtures. Knead well, cover with a piece of oiled polythene and leave for ¾–1 hour to double in size. Turn on to a floured board and knead again. Divide into small pieces and form into fingers. Place fairly close together on greased baking-trays, cover with oiled polythene and leave to rise for 20–30 minutes. Brush with beaten egg and sprinkle with a little salt. Bake at 425°F/Gas 7 for 15 minutes. Cool, wrap and freeze.

To serve:
Allow to thaw out for about 15 minutes at room temperature or heat in the oven for about 5 minutes.

Victoria Sandwich Cake

4-ounce margarine
4-ounce caster sugar
2 eggs
4-ounce self-raising flour
1 tablespoon warm water

Freezer Storage Life: up to 6 months

Preparation for freezing:
Grease and line 2-7-inch sandwich-tins.
Cream the margarine with the sugar until light and fluffy. Beat in the eggs, one at a time, then fold in the flour and stir in the water. Spoon the mixture into the prepared tins and bake at 375°F/Gas 5 for 20–25 minutes until firm in the centre. Turn out on to cooling trays.
The layers can be filled with butter cream, then placed in the freezer until hard, wrapped and returned to the freezer.
If frozen with no filling, place a piece of foil or moisture- and vapour-proof paper between the layers then wrap.

To serve:
Remove from freezer and leave for 2–3 hours to thaw.

Variations
Chocolate: Instead of using 4 ounces flour, sieve 1 ounce cocoa with 3 ounces flour and add 2–3 drops vanilla essence.

Cherry and almond: Use 3 ounces flour and add 4 ounces chopped glacé cherries, 2 ounces ground almonds and 2–3 drops almond essence.

Coffee and walnut: Dissolve 3 teaspoons instant coffee in the warm water and add 2 ounces chopped walnuts.

Mixed fruit: Add 4 ounces sultanas, 2 ounces currants, 1 ounce mixed peel and 1 teaspoon mixed spice.

Glacé Fruit Cake

8-ounce butter
8-ounce caster sugar
½ teaspoon almond essence
3 eggs
8-ounce plain flour
pinch salt
4-ounce ground almonds
4-ounce glacé cherries (chopped)
2-ounce mixed peel
6-ounce glacé pineapple (chopped)
1-ounce crystallised ginger (chopped)
2-ounce angelica (chopped)
1 tablespoon brandy

Freezer Storage Life: up to 6 months

Preparation for freezing:
Grease and line an 8-inch cake-tin.
Cream the butter and sugar until light and fluffy and add the vanilla essence. Beat in the eggs, one at a time. Fold in the flour, ground almonds and fruits, and stir in the brandy.
Place in the prepared tin and bake at 275°F/Gas 1 for 3–3½ hours. Turn out and cool. Wrap and freeze.

To serve:
Allow the cake to thaw out for at least 8 hours.

Sponge Sandwich

3 eggs
3-ounce caster sugar
3-ounce plain flour
pinch salt
1 tablespoon warm water

Freezer Storage Life: up to 6 months

Preparation for freezing:
Grease and flour 2–7-inch sandwich-tins.
Whisk eggs and sugar in a basin over a saucepan of hot water until thick and creamy. Sieve flour and salt and fold half into the eggs and sugar. Stir in the warm water and fold in remaining flour. Spoon into the prepared tins and bake at 400°F/ Gas 6 for 18–20 minutes until firm to the touch. Cool on a wire rack. Place a piece of foil between each layer, then wrap and freeze.

To serve:
Allow to thaw out at room temperature for 1–2 hours. Fill with fresh whipped cream or butter cream.

Lemon Chiffon Cake

9-ounce self-raising flour
6-ounce caster sugar
pinch salt
grated rind 1 lemon
6 eggs
8 tablespoons oil
5 tablespoons water

Filling:
4-ounce butter
8-ounce icing sugar
1 teaspoon grated lemon rind
1 tablespoon lemon juice
Freezer Storage Life: up to 6 months

Preparation for freezing:
Grease and line an 8-inch cake-tin.
Mix the flour, rind, sugar and salt in a basin.
Separate the eggs and add the egg yolks, oil and
water to the dry ingredients. Beat well until
smooth. Whisk the egg whites until stiff and fold
into the cake mixture. Spoon into the prepared tin
and bake at 325°F/Gas 3 for 20–30 minutes until
firm. Turn out and cool on a wire rack.
For filling:
Cream the butter and icing sugar until light and
fluffy, add lemon rind and juice.
Cut the cake in half and sandwich with half the
filling. Spread the other half of filling on the top.
Place in the freezer until hard then wrap and
freeze.
To serve:
Allow to thaw out for about 3 hours.

Tea-time Scones

12-ounce self-raising flour
pinch salt
4-ounce butter *or* margarine
3-ounce caster sugar
1 egg
milk to mix
Freezer Storage Life: up to 6 months

Preparation for freezing:
Sieve flour and salt into a basin, rub in the butter
or margarine until the mixture resembles fine
breadcrumbs. Add sugar and mix in the egg and

enough milk to give a fairly soft (but manageable)
consistency. Turn the dough out on to a floured
board and knead lightly. Roll out to ¼-inch thickness and cut into rounds. Place on greased baking-
trays and bake at 400°F/Gas 6 for 10–15 minutes.
Cool, wrap and freeze.
To serve:
Allow to thaw out at room temperature for about
1 hour or while frozen heat through in the oven
for 10 minutes. Serve with butter and jam.

Variations
Fruit scones: Add 3 ounces mixed dried fruit to
the above mixture.

Cheese scones: Omit the sugar and add 3 ounces
grated cheese to the dry mix.

Quick and Easy Doughnuts

8-ounce plain flour
2 teaspoons baking powder
2-ounce butter *or* margarine
2-ounce caster sugar
2 eggs
jam
Freezer Storage Life: up to 3 months

Preparation for freezing:
Sieve the flour and baking powder into a basin.
Rub in the butter or margarine and add the sugar.
Lightly beat the eggs and stir into the dry ingredients, add a little milk if necessary to make a
fairly stiff dough. Roll out to a ¼-inch thickness
and cut into rounds. Place a little jam in the centre
of half the rounds, brush edges with milk, and
place the other rounds on top. Press edges with a
fork to seal. Fry in deep oil until risen and a
golden brown. Drain on kitchen paper and dredge
with caster sugar. Cool, wrap and freeze.
To serve:
Allow to thaw out at room temperature for 2–3
hours or if preferred hot, place in the oven for
15–20 minutes.

Plain White Bread

½-ounce fresh *or* ¼-ounce dried yeast
1 teaspoon sugar
¼ pint milk and water (mixed)
1-pound strong flour
1 teaspoon salt
2-ounce lard *or* margarine

Freezer Storage Life: up to 2 months

Preparation for freezing:
Grease a 2-pound loaf-tin.
Blend the fresh yeast with the sugar and mix with the milk, or sprinkle the dried yeast on to the milk and sugar and leave for 10 minutes until frothy. Sieve the flour and salt and rub in the lard or margarine. Mix in the yeast mixture; if the mixture is too dry add a little extra milk. Knead the dough until firm and smooth, cover with a piece of oiled polythene and leave to prove, i.e. until risen to twice its size. Turn on to a floured board and knead the dough again. Form into a shape the size of the tin, place dough in the tin and leave to rise (covered with oiled polythene) for about 30 minutes until the dough has risen to the rim of the tin. Brush with milk and bake at 425°F/Gas 7 for 20–25 minutes then reduce heat to 350°F/Gas 4 for a further 15–20 minutes. To test if the loaf is cooked, tap the base and if it sounds 'hollow' it is cooked. Cool, wrap and freeze.

To serve:
Allow to thaw out overnight in the refrigerator or for about 4–5 hours at room temperature. If required in a hurry, wrap the loaf in foil and heat through in the oven.

Wholemeal Bread

1-ounce fresh *or* ½-ounce dried yeast
½-ounce sugar
½ pint warm water
1-ounce butter
1-pound wholemeal flour
½ tablespoon salt

Freezer Storage Life: up to 2 months

Preparation for freezing:
Grease a 2-pound loaf-tin.
Prepare the yeast as for plain white bread. Rub the butter into the flour and salt, add the yeast mixture and continue method for white bread. Bake at 450°F/Gas 8 for 15 minutes then reduce temperature to 400°F/Gas 6 for 20–30 minutes.

To serve:
As for plain white bread.

Yorkshire Parkin

4-ounce plain flour
8-ounce medium oatmeal
1-ounce sugar
pinch salt
½ teaspoon ground ginger
5-ounce treacle
4-ounce golden syrup
4-ounce butter
½ teaspoon bicarbonate of soda
2 fluid-ounce milk (warmed)

Freezer Storage Life: up to 6 months

Preparation for freezing:
Grease and flour an 8-inch cake-tin.
Mix flour, oatmeal, sugar, salt and ginger in a basin. Place the treacle, syrup and butter in a saucepan and heat until the butter is dissolved. Dissolve the bicarbonate of soda in the warm milk. Pour the melted mixture and milk on to the dry ingredients and mix well. Pour into the prepared tin and bake at 325°F/Gas 3 for 45–50 minutes. Turn out and cool on a wire rack. Wrap and freeze.

To serve:
Allow to thaw out at room temperature for about 5 hours.

Danish Pastries

1-ounce fresh *or* ½-ounce dried yeast
¼ pint milk (warmed)
1 teaspoon sugar
1-pound plain flour
1 teaspoon salt
10-ounce butter
2-ounce caster sugar
2 eggs

Fillings:—see below
beaten egg to glaze

Freezer Storage Life: up to 3 months

Preparation for freezing:
Dissolve the fresh yeast in the milk and sugar or sprinkle dried yeast on to the milk and sugar and leave for 10 minutes until frothy. Sieve the flour and salt, rub in 2 ounces of the butter and add 2 ounces caster sugar. Add the yeast liquid and eggs and mix well to make a soft dough (add more milk if necessary). Cover and leave in the refrigerator for 10 minutes.

Allow remaining butter to slightly soften and form into an oblong 9 × 5 inches. Turn the dough out on to a floured board, knead lightly until smooth and roll to an oblong 12 × 8 inches. Place the butter in the centre and fold the edges of the dough over to completely enclose the butter. Roll out the dough to a strip about 5 × 15 inches. Fold the bottom third up and the top third down, cover and leave to 'rest' in the refrigerator for 10 minutes. Repeat the rolling process twice more. Cover and leave in the refrigerator while making the fillings.

To shape:
1. Roll out the dough and cut into 3-inch squares, place filling in the centre, brush edges with beaten egg, and fold in half to make either oblong or triangular 'cushions'.

2. Roll out the dough and cut into 3-inch squares, place filling in the centre, brush edges with beaten egg and bring the 4 corners into the centre.

3. Roll dough into an oblong 12 × 6 inches, spread with filling. Roll up like a swiss roll and cut into 1-inch slices.

Fillings for Danish Pastries

Almond paste:
Cream ½ ounce butter with 3 ounces caster sugar. Mix in 3 ounces ground almonds, 2–3 drops almond essence and a little beaten egg to make a firm paste.

Confectioner's custard:
Blend 1 ounce flour, 1 ounce caster sugar and 1 egg with 2 tablespoons from ¼ pint milk. Bring the rest of the milk to the boil, add to the blended mixture, stirring all the time, then return to the pan. Bring gently to the boil and cook, stirring, for 2 minutes. Add 2–3 drops vanilla essence. Cool.

Cinnamon sugar:
Cream 2 ounces butter with 2 ounces caster sugar and stir in 2 teaspoons ground cinnamon.

Apricot apple:
Peel and thinly slice 2 eating apples, sprinkle with a little lemon juice and stir in 3–4 tablespoons apricot jam.

To finish the pastries:
After the pastries have been shaped, place on greased baking-trays and leave for 20–30 minutes. Glaze with beaten egg and bake at 425°F/Gas 7 for 15 minutes. Cool and coat with a little glacé icing. Place in freezer until hard, then wrap and freeze.

To serve:
Allow to thaw out at room temperature for 2–3 hours or if preferred warm, place on a baking-tray, cover with foil and heat through in the oven for 10–15 minutes.

Rum Babas

$\frac{1}{4}$-ounce dried yeast
1 teaspoon sugar
$\frac{1}{8}$ pint warm water
4$\frac{1}{2}$-ounce plain flour
pinch salt
1 egg
1-ounce butter (melted)
1-2-ounce currants

To serve:
6-ounce sugar
$\frac{1}{3}$ pint water
juice $\frac{1}{2}$ lemon
rum or rum essence
double cream
Freezer Storage Life: up to 3 months

Preparation for freezing:
Grease 6 individual ring moulds.
Sprinkle the yeast with sugar into the warm water and leave for 10 minutes until frothy. Sieve flour and salt together, add yeast liquid, egg and butter and beat well until smooth.
Place the currants into each ring mould and pour the batter into each one. Leave in a warm place for about 20 minutes until the mixture rises to the top of the tins. Bake at 425°F/Gas 7 for 15-20 minutes. Remove from tins, cool, wrap and freeze.

To serve:
Allow the babas to thaw out for about 1 hour at room temperature. Meanwhile make the syrup— boil the sugar and water for 5 minutes, then stir in lemon juice and rum to taste. Cool slightly and pour over the babas (do this slowly to allow the syrup to soak through) cool and decorate with whipped cream.

Fruit Savarin

Make double the above mixture and bake in a 10-inch savarin tin at 400°F/Gas 6. Pour over the syrup and fill the centre with drained canned fruits.

Freezer Storage Life: up to 3 months

INDEX

JULY

Fish
Bream
Crab
Dab
Hake
Halibut
Herring
Lobster
Grey and
  Red Mullet
Plaice
Prawns
Salmon
Shrimps
Sole
Sea Trout

Fruit
Apricot
Bilberry
Blackcurrant
Cherry
Gooseberry
Loganberry
Peach
Plum
Raspberry
Redcurrant
Strawberry
Game
Venison
**Meat and
  Poultry**
Lamb

Vegetables
Globe
  Artichoke
Asparagus
Aubergine
Broad and
  French Beans
Runner Beans
New Carrots
Cauliflower
Corn-on-
  the-Cob
Courgettes
Mange-tout
  peas
Peas
Spinach
Tomatoes

AUGUST

Fish
Bream
Crab
Dab
Hake
Halibut
Herring
Lobster
Grey and
  Red Mullet
Plaice
Prawns
Salmon
Shrimps
Sole
Sea Trout
Turbot

Fruit
Apple
Apricot
Blackberry
Blackcurrant
Cherry
Damson
Gooseberry
Loganberry
Peach
Pear
Plum
Raspberry
Redcurrant
Strawberry
Game
Blackcock
Grouse
Ptarmigan
Quail
Venison

**Meat and
  Poultry**
Lamb
Vegetables
Globe
  Artichoke
Aubergine
Broad and
  French Beans
Runner Beans
Cabbage
Cauliflower
Corn-on-
  the-Cob
Courgettes
Mange-tout
  peas
Peas
Spinach
Tomatoes

SEPTEMBER

Fish
Bream
Brill
Crab
Dab
Haddock
Hake
Halibut
Herring
Lobster
Grey and
  Red Mullet
Oysters
Plaice
Salmon
Sole
Turbot

Fruit
Apple
Blackberry
Damson
Greengage
Peach
Pear
Plum
Game
Blackcock
Grouse
Hare
Partridge
Ptarmigan
Quail
Rabbit
Venison
Wild Duck
  and Goose
Scottish
  Woodcock

**Meat and
  Poultry**
Scotch Beef
Goose
Lamb
Turkey
Vegetables
Globe
  Artichoke
Aubergine
Cabbage
Cauliflower
Celeriac
Celery
Courgettes
Field
  Mushrooms
Spinach